JÜRGEN WERBICK

GOD'S WEAKNESS FOR HUMANKIND

Pope Francis' view of God

LIBERIA EDITRICE VATICANA

Published in Australia by

© Copyright 2019 Coventry Press

Coventry Press
33 Scoresby Road
Bayswater Vic. 3153
Australia

Original title: *Gottes Schwäche für den Menschen*

Translated from German by Fabrizio Iodice
Translated into English by Salesians of Don Bosco of the Province of Mary Help of Christians of Australia and the Pacific

ISBN 9780987643131

© Copyright 2017 - Libreria Editrice Vaticana
00120 Città del Vaticano
Tel. 06.698.81032 - Fax 06.698.84716
commerciale.lev@spc.va

All rights reserved. Other than for the purposes and subject to the conditions prescribed under the *Copyright Act*, no part of this publication may be reproduced, stored in a retrieval system, or transmitted in any form or by any means, electronic, mechanical, photocopying, recording or otherwise, without the prior permission of the publisher.

Cataloguing-in-Publication entry is available from the National Library of Australia http:/catalogue.nla.gov.au/.

Printed in Australia

www.coventrypress.com.au

SERIES
THE THEOLOGY OF POPE FRANCIS

JURGEN WERBICK: *God's Weakness for Humankind.* Pope Francis' view of God

LUCIO CASULA: *Faces, Gestures and Places.* Pope Francis' Christology

PETER HÜNERMANN: *Human Beings According to Christ Today.* Pope Francis' Anthropology

ROBERTO REPOLE: *The Dream of a Gospel-inspired Church.* Pope Francis' Ecclesiology

CARLOS GALLI: *Christ, Mary, the Church and the Peoples.* Pope Francis' Mariology

SANTIAGO MADRIGAL TERRAZAS: *'Unity Prevails over Conflict'.* Pope Francis' Ecumenism

ARISTIDE FUMAGALLI: *Journeying in Love.* Pope Francis' Moral Theology

JUAN CARLOS SCANNONE: *The Gospel of Mercy in the Spirit of Discernment.* Pope Francis' Social Ethics

MARINELLA PERRONI: *Kerygma and Prophecy.* Pope Francis' Biblical Hermeneutics

PIERO CODA: *'The Church is the Gospel'.* At the sources of Pope Francis' theology

MARKO IVAN RUPNIK: *According to the Spirit.* Spiritual theology on the move with Pope Francis' Church

ABBREVIATIONS

AL	*Amoris Laetitia*
EG	*Evangelii Gaudium*
EN	*Evangelii Nuntiandi*
GS	*Gaudium et Spes*
LG	*Lumen Gentium*
LS	*Laudato Si'*
MeM	*Misericordia et Misera*
RS	*Ratio Studiorum*
SE	*Spiritual Exercises*

PREFACE TO THE SERIES

From the time of his first appearance in St Peter's Square on the evening of his election, it was more than clear that Francis' pontificate would be adopting a new style. His modest apparel, calling himself the Bishop of Rome, asking the people to pray for him – in the 'deafening silence' of a packed square – and greeting them with a simple '*buonasera*' (good evening) ... these were all eloquent signs of the fact that there was a change taking place in the way the Pope related to people, and thus in the 'language' used.

The gestures and words that have followed from that occasion only confirm and strengthen this first impression. Indeed, it could be said that over the ensuing years, the image of the papacy has been decidedly transformed, involving a change that affects homilies, addresses and documents promulgated as well.

As could be predicted, this has generated divergent opinions, especially regarding his teaching. While many have in fact welcomed his magisterium with enthusiasm and deep interest, sensing the fresh wind of the gospel, some others have approached it in a more detached way and, at times, with suspicion. There has been no lack of more absolute views, even going as far as to doubt the existence of a theology in Francis' teaching.

A summary judgement of this kind could come from the very different backgrounds of Francis and his predecessor, Benedict XVI. The latter, we know, has been one of the most outstanding and important theologians of the twentieth century and undoubtedly relied on his personal theological development in his rich papal magisterium. We have not yet fully appreciated, nor will we cease to appreciate, the depth of this magisterium. What Bergoglio has behind him, on the other hand, is his long and deep-rooted experience as a religious and a pastor.

However, this does not mean that his magisterium is without a theology. The fact that he was not mostly, or only, a 'professional' theologian does not mean that his magisterium is not supported by a theology. Were this the case, we could say that, strictly speaking, the majority of his predecessors were without a theology, given that Ratzinger represents the exception rather than the rule.

In any case, the fact that we can discuss the theological significance of Francis' magisterium, as well as the fact that, very often, some of his highly evocative and very immediate expressions have been so abused as to rob them of their profundity – in the journalistic as well as the ecclesial ambit – makes the response of this series, which I have the honour of presenting, a significant one.

By drawing on the competence and rigorous study of theologians of proven worth, coming from diverse contexts, the series has sought to research the theological thinking which supports the Pope's teaching. It explores its roots, its freshness, and its continuity with earlier magisterium.

The result can be found in the eleven volumes which make up this series with its simple and direct title: 'The Theology of Pope Francis'.

They can be read independently of one another, obviously; they have been written by individual authors independently of each other. Nevertheless, the hope is that a reading of the entire series would not only be a valuable aid for grasping the theology upon which Francis' teaching is based, in the various theological fields of knowledge, but also an introduction to the key points of his thinking and teaching overall.

The intention, then, is not one of 'apologetics', and even less so is it to add further voices to the many already speaking about the Pope. The aim is to try to see, and to help others to see, what theological thinking Francis bases himself on and expresses, in such a fresh way in his teaching.

Among the many discoveries the reader could make in reading these volumes, would certainly be that of observing how so much of the beneficial freshness of the Council's teaching flows into Francis' magisterium. This is true both of the theological preparation he has had, and of what has followed from it. Given that it is perhaps still too soon for all this wealth to become common patrimony, peacefully and fully received by everyone, it should be no surprise that the Pope's teaching is sometimes not immediately understood by everyone.

By the same token, a point of no return has been reached in Francis' teaching, one that recent theology and the Council have both taught: that doctrine cannot be something extraneous to so-called pastoral theology and ministry. The truth that the Church is called to watch over is the truth of Christ's gospel, which needs to be communicated to the women and men of every time and place. This is why the task of the ecclesial magisterium must also be one of favouring this communication of the gospel. Hence, theology can never be reduced to a dry, desk-bound exercise, disconnected from the life of the people of God and its mission. This mission is that the women and men of every age encounter the perennial and inexhaustible freshness of Jesus' gospel.

Over these years there have been those who have heard some of Francis' own critical statements regarding theology or theologians, and have concluded that he holds it and them in low esteem. Perhaps a more detailed study of the Pope's teaching, such as offered by this series, could also be helpful for showing that, while we always need to be critical of a theology that loses its vital connection to the living faith of the Church, it is also essential to have a theology which takes up the task of thinking critically about this very faith, and doing so with 'creative fidelity', so that it may continue to be proclaimed.

Francis' teaching is certainly not lacking in a theology of this kind; and a theology of the kind is certainly one much desired by a magisterium such as his, which so wants God's mercy to continue to touch the minds and hearts of the women and men of our time.

Editor-in-chief
ROBERTO REPOLE

CONTENTS

Abbreviations 4
Preface to the Series 5

Chapter 1
"The glory of God is the living man" (Irenaeus of Lyon)............................11

Chapter 2
God the Creator and his passion for what he has created......................23

Chapter 3
God's gift — God's challenge 31

Chapter 4
Justice-as-gift 45

Chapter 5
God is merciful 57

Chapter 6
God's mercy is the soul of justice....................69

Chapter 7
The face of God's mercy 79

Chapter 8
Mercy which proves God's omnipotence 87

Chapter 9
The mystery of God's love: the Trinity 99

Chapter 1
"THE GLORY OF GOD IS THE LIVING MAN"
(IRENAEUS OF LYON)

Irenaeus, arguably the most important theologian of the second century, offered an early insight in the above quote which has become a point of reference for Christianity of both the West and the East. It it a valid summary, too, of how Pope Francis wants theological discourse focused on God to be seen. To speak of God it is necessary to speak of the human being and of how his or her life develops according to genuine human nature. But to speak of the human being and the fullness of human life, it is necessary to speak of God. First of all, then, the notion should be spread that: 'Anyone who excludes God from his horizons falsifies the notion of "reality" and, as a consequence, can only end up in blind alleys or with recipes for destruction.'[1] Political ideas and ideological approaches which put God in parentheses have so often proven their inhumanity.[2] An 'exclusive humanism' (Charles Taylor) began in the 17th

---

1 From Pope Benedict XVI's opening address to the 5th General Assembly of the Latin American and Caribbean Episcopate at Aparecida, 13 May 2007.

2 According to the *Concluding Document of the 5th General Assembly at Aparecida* (no. 405). Cardinal Bergoglio played a key role in drafting this document. In the remainder of our text, recent documents of ecclesial magisterium are indicated with abbreviation and number, following the *Acta Apostolicae Sedis*.

century with the ever-increasing determination that people could pursue their highest goals and commitments 'without God coming into play'; he also regarded 'moral and spiritual resources' as something 'purely immanent.'[3] This has proven to be deeply ambivalent, and not only since the collapse of real socialism.

It cannot be denied, of course, that this exclusive anthropocentrism was also the result of it being the common view that one had to defend oneself against a theocentric theology which erroneously excluded whatever is human. The orientation of human life to God and eschatological salvation was understood as a necessary step to achieve original human needs and concerns. It seemed to many as if human beings had to say 'No' to the fulfilment of life in this world if they wanted to believe in God and the call to eternal beatitude. God and the world, a life dedicated to God's Lordship and the joy of living in this world, were perceived as opposites in the face of which one had to choose the one and deny the other.

The *mutual exclusion* between belief in God and 'secularity' went back to a deep misunderstanding of the constitutive element of Christianity, especially of Jesus Christ's proclamation that God's kingdom was near, and indeed had already arrived among believers. This misunderstanding

---

[3] Cf. C TAYLOR, *A Secular Age*, Harvard University Press 2007. The German edition is quoted here, from *Ein säkulares Zeitalter,* Suhrkamp, Frankfurt a.M. 2009, 401 ff. or also 418. In his book, Taylor outlined in a precise and detailed manner how this culture of unbridled humanism gained plausibility for its so-called 'self-sufficiency'.

has profoundly marked and compromised the situation of the faith, at least in Europe and America since the Enlightenment. No one has succeeded in expressing this more provocatively than the German philosopher Friedrich Nietzsche. For him, the Christian God is *'the enemy of life'*,[4] *'degenerated into the contradiction* of life, instead of being transfiguration and an eternal Yes.' This 'eternal Yes' to life would be, in Nietzsche's view, the view of the classical philologists, the epitome of the pagan religion. He shows contempt for Christianity and its 'God on the Cross': 'In him war is declared on life, on nature, on the will to live! God becomes the formula for every slander upon the "here and now," and for every lie about the "beyond"! In him nothingness is deified, and the will to nothingness is made holy!... This is how far we have come! ... Do you not know it yet? Christianity is a nihilistic religion – for the sake of its God ...'[5] Nietzsche contrasts this Christianity with his Dionysian religion: ' – Have I been understood? – Dionysus against the Crucified ...'[6] Zarathustra, the 'prophet' of this religion, invites his disciples to pursue their way:

> I beseech you, my brothers, remain faithful to
> the earth, and do not believe those who speak
> to you of otherworldly hopes! Poison-mixers are

---

[4] *Götzen-Dämmerung* (Twilight of the Idols), Friedrich Nietzsche, *Sämtliche Werke, Kritische Studienausgabe* (KSA), G. Colli – M. Montinari (eds.), Deutscher Taschenbuchverlag, Munich – Berlin/New York 1980, Vol. 6, 85.

[5] Cf. FRIEDRICH NIETZSCHE, *Nachgelassene Fragmente Mai–Juni 1888*, 17 [4], KSA 13, 525.

[6] Cf. FRIEDRICH NIETZSCHE *Ecce homo. Warum ich ein Schicksal bin* 9, KSA 6, 374.

> they, whether they know it or not. Despisers of life are they, decaying and poisoned themselves, of whom the earth is weary: so let them go.
>
> Once the sin against God was the greatest sin; but God died, and these sinners died with him. To sin against the earth is now the most dreadful thing, and to esteem the entrails of the unknowable higher than the meaning of the earth.[7]

Nietzsche's 'Curse on Christianity'[8] can be largely explained by his life-story of faith or lack of it. But it found tremendous response among intellectuals, since, among other things, Christian preaching against the pride of 'enlightened' citizens of the world was only able to talk about the failure of a secular search for happiness and success.[9] Thus a culture of religious scepticism developed amongst the 'educated' middle-class and also among the working class – who were given little consideration by the Church – as a result of a consciously adopted worldliness

---

7 Cf. FRIEDRICH NIETZSCHE, *Also sprach Zarathustra*, Zarathustra's Vorrede 3, KSA 4, 15. [*Thus Spake Zarathustra*, is available in the public domain in the Gutenberg.org online collection].

8 So reads the subtitle of his last work *Der Antichrist*, KSA 6, 165. [*The Anti-Christ*, also available in the public domain].

9 B GROETHUYSEN, *Die Entstehung der bürglichen Welt- und Lebensanschauung in Frankreich (*The Origin of the Bourgeois World and Life in France), 2 vols, reprint of the first edition of 1927, Fischer, Frankfurt a.M. 1978, conveys an impression of this fatal homiletic strategy documented with many preaching texts from before the French Revolution.

suspicious of Christianity *en bloc*, for having fossilized into hostility towards the world.[10]

Christian contexts and popular piety which have had little contact over a lengthy period with this culture of excluding God, have been largely immune to this criticism of Christianity up until now. But the enormous increase in mobility, and finally, the overcoming of boundaries of all contexts through digital network communication, have certainly contributed to the fact that themes of criticism of Christianity and God became accessible everywhere in the 20th century and have been taken up precisely where local churches were strongly tied to power and business elites. These elites were very interested in the 'otherworldly perspective' [*Verjenseitigung*] of the belief in God, so that on the 'earthly' [*Diesseits*] side, everything could remain as it was as far as possible – in their favour. But Karl Marx's famous description of religion as 'the opium of the people'[11]

---

10 I found an important expression, which then became a proverbial one, regarding this self-conscious cultural criticism of Christianity in H HEINE, *A Winter's Tale*, Chapter 1, where it says: "A new song, a better song, My friends will be my aim! / We should, right now on earth, / A kingdom of heaven proclaim … Enough bread grows here on earth, / For all mankind's nutrition, / Roses too, myrtles, beauty and joy, / And green peas, in addition. *Yes, green peas for everyone,* As soon as they burst their pods. / To the angels and the sparrows, / We leave Heaven and its Gods."
Sigmund Freud took up this theme in his important work on the analysis of religion, *Die Zukunft einer Illusion aufgenommen*; cf. Id., *Studienausgabe*, A MITSCHERLICH-A RICHARDS-J STRACHEY (eds.), Vol IX: *Fragen der Gesellschaft. Ursprünge der Religion*, Fischer, Frankfurt a. M. 1974, 135–189, 183.

11 K MARX, *Zur Kritik der Hegelschen Rechtsphilosophie. Einleitung*, in Marx–Engels–Werke, Vol. 1, Dietz, Berlin 1970,

was then understood by theology and faith awareness, especially after the Second Vatican Council, as a wake-up call for rejecting the fact that Christian belief in God could serve the interests of oppressors and exploiters, stressing the fact that believers are called to work for liberation in the world.

Urged on by an understanding of the Second Vatican Council's Pastoral Constitution *Gaudium et Spes* (*GS*), and in continuity with it, various currents of a *theology of liberation* emerged in Latin America. Sometimes these resorted to Marxist analyses to counter the temptation of Christian belief in God to otherworldliness, and to place the focus in theology on the encounter with God or Christ which occurs when we encounter the poor, and when we are in solidarity with the 'crucified peoples.'[12] The *theology of the people*, as it developed at the same time, especially in Argentina, also understood itself as liberation theology, but set itself more clearly against approaches tied to Marxist analysis. It was committed to the option for the poor, and popular religion, and saw the liberating encounter with God in the challenge of the poor. Jorge Mario Bergoglio was and is close to this theology. As Pope Francis, he has often taken up its approach in sermons and documents. Again and again he comes back to this central idea, as a leitmotiv of his

---

378–391, re, p. 378. It was Lenin who then described religion as the opium of the people: administered by those who were interested in diverting the oppressed from their suffering.

12 Typical is I. ELLACURIA-J. SOBRINO (eds.) *Mysterium Liberationis. Grundbegriffe der Theologie der Befreiung*, dt. Exodus, Luzern 1995/1996.

discourse about God: God is and wants *inclusion*; he brings this about in and with human beings, and together with them wants to bring about inclusion of the *excluded* so that everyone has a share in the fullness of life. The fundamental danger of our culture is therefore exclusion, including in the sense of an everyday cultural exclusion of God caused by the indifference of believers towards those in need: 'Whenever the least of our brothers and sisters finds a place in our hearts, it is God himself who finds a place there. When that brother or sister is shut out, it is God himself who is not being welcomed.'[13]

The metaphors of exclusion/inclusion and insertion/inclusion can be instructive in many ways for how we speak about God today. I want to give them a key hermeneutic function in outlining and contextualizing Pope Francis' 'doctrine' regarding God; also for their impact on fundamental theology and fundamental pastoral theology, spirituality, and their reference to key topics in dogmatic theology.[14]

13   Homily on 23 February 2014 at the Concistory for new cardinals (http.//w2.vatican.va/content/francesco/en/homilies/2014/documents/papa-francesco_omelia-nuovi-cardinali.html).

14   It is characteristic of the theology of the people inspired especially by *Lucio Gera*, that these dimensions of discourse about God can only be developed contextually. On Gera, cf. M ECKHOLT, „... *bei mir erwächst die Theologie aus der Pastoral. Lucio Gera – ein „Lehrer der Theologie" von Papst Franziskus, in: Stimmen der Zeit* 232 (2014), 157–172. Cf. L GERA, *Evangelisierung und Förderung des Menschen*, in P HÜNERMANN-JC SCANNONE (eds.), *Lateinamerika und die katholische Soziallehre: ein deutsch-lateinamerikanisches Dialogprogramm*, Part 1: *Wissenschaft und kulturelle Praxis, Evangelisierung*, Grünewald, Mainz 1989, 245–299.

The orientation of his doctrine of God where fundamental theology and fundamental pastoral theology are concerned is determined by his belief that there is a contradiction in mutual exclusion between our relationship with God and the presence of human beings in the world, as has been established since the European Enlightenment, at least in the intellectual culture of the West. *GS* 38 provided the perspective, as it speaks of the presence of the Church in the world as its fundamental vocation, and understands this vocation to come from the incarnation of the Word:

> For God's Word, through Whom all things were made, was Himself made flesh and dwelt on the earth of men. Thus He entered the world's history as a perfect man, taking that history up into Himself and summarizing it. He Himself revealed to us that "God is love" (1 John 4:8) and at the same time taught us that the new command of love was the basic law of human perfection and hence of the worlds transformation. To those, therefore, who believe in divine love, He gives assurance that the way of love lies open to men and that the effort to establish a universal brotherhood is not a hopeless one.

The incarnate presence of the Word of God in the world is the measure for the Church's mission. It should be, like the mission of the *Logos* made flesh, a presence of service for people to know and to grasp his existence out of love and their vocation to share in God's love which brings the world to perfection.[15] In Jesus Christ, God reveals to human beings their humanity and the divine dignity proper to it. So all Christian discourse about God starts here. And from here must come a reflection that includes this insight into the eternal dignity of human beings as well as their commitment to it. John Paul II succinctly expresses this fundamental theological and pastoral intention in his post-synodal letter *Ecclesia in America* (*EA*, no. 27, January 22, 1999): 'Jesus is the human face of God and the divine face of man.'[16]

It is only possible to speak of God from a Christian point of view if this discourse consistently aligns with God's self-revelation in Jesus Christ. The *idea* of God has to refer to this *reality* of God, should *reflect* on it[17] to enlighten it in faith and to relate it to the reality of human life in the world and in history. Also, and especially true for reflection on God, is the principle that 'conceptual tools exist to heighten contact with the realities they seek to explain, not to distance us from them' (*Evangelii Gaudium* no. 194, *EG*). But especially in view of the history of theology, it is hard to avoid this critical insight: ideas disconnected from realities give rise to ineffectual forms of idealism and nominalism, capable at most of classifying and defining, but certainly not calling to action. What calls us to action are realities illuminated by reason' (*EG*, nos 194 and 232). The human being is

15 Cf. no. 3 of *GS* which alludes to Mk 10:44-35.
16 The same line is picked in *Aparecida*, no. 392
17 This is spelt out in one of Pope Francis' main guidelines, something he repeats often: 'Realities are more important than ideas' (*EG*, no. 231; *Laudato Si'*, no. 110).

queried and challenged to the depths of his or her existence by the reality of God, as encountered in Jesus Christ and grasped through the Holy Spirit. Human beings expose themselves to this reality when they allow God's *Logos* to speak within them, as it was spoken and as it took form in the life of Jesus Christ. God's *Logos* speaks where people perceive the face of God in Jesus Christ: God's challenging presence in the human world. Very concretely, God's *Logos* speaks and can be understood in those whom Jesus Christ wants to encounter here and now: in the poor and excluded who invite their brothers and sisters – brothers and sisters of Jesus Christ – to open themselves to God's kingdom by opening themselves to the suffering of the 'little ones' (Cf. Mt 25: 31-46).

Their *reality* shows the divine face of human beings; it shows human beings who share in the life in which God sets his 'glory'. When human beings recognize this reality, as the brothers or sisters of Christ, it is as God wants these 'little ones' to be recognized and honoured. The encounter with God and Christ in the poor reveals their 'divine countenance'. It is a reality which urges all who are touched in the depths of their vocation and divine dignity by embracing this encounter, to give witness to the poor of God's good wish as Creator: that he himself become a reality in a world which humiliates and shows contempt for human beings.

God's reality confronts human beings with their reality of being human. God does not want to be sought out and found otherwise. Human beings are in God's image. His

Christ is the icon of God in whom people should know who and how God is.[18] Christ is 'the face of God ... through whom God is made visible and revealed.[19] The poor and excluded are in God's image and his living request not to be dishonoured in them. Believers are in God's image; and they are all the more so the more – by the grace of Christ – that God's good will is shown through them and becomes a reality in the world.

This is the framework of a doctrine of God as it can be articulated from the liberation theology of the people and in many of the documents and expressions of this man of the Church, Jorge Mario Bergoglio, and ultimately therefore, of Pope Francis.

---

18 The Son 'is the reflection of God's glory and the exact imprint of God's very being' (Heb 1:3), is the 'image of the invisible God' (Col 1:15).

19 CLEMENT OF ALEXANDRIA, *Paidogogos* 1, 57, 2.

CHAPTER 2
GOD THE CREATOR AND HIS PASSION FOR WHAT HE HAS CREATED

When speaking of the human being as an image of God, reference is first of all made to God's work of creation, as witnessed in the first chapters of the book of Genesis. The Hebrew words *(ṣelem, demûth)* used here (Gen 1:26-27) along with their contexts, characterize human beings as collaborators of God in his creation.[1] They should not subjugate the earth to their rule, but bring it to fruition and enjoy it. Creation is both a good gift to human beings and a challenging task; it is entrusted to people's care so that it remains God's gift, as the Encyclical *Laudato Si'* insists on in the face of environmental degradation.

When humanity is mentioned in this sense as the collaborator of the Creator God, this presupposes a theology of creation which understands creation as a process initiated and sustained by God, as *creatio continua seu continuata*. This corresponds to the insights of modern theories of evolution, but is certainly anchored in Christian beliefs themselves. For the Jesuit Pope Francis, the theologoumenon of *creatio ex nihilo* takes on a central Ignatian spiritual and

---

1 Cf. *LS*, no. 117 with reference to the Encyclical *Centesimus Annus*, 1 May 1991, no. 37, by John Paul II.

ethical theological significance. Ignatius of Loyola, in the 'Contemplation to attain the love of God' in his *Spiritual Exercises*, opened up a spiritual perspective on creation which seems quite astonishing for his time and leads to an experience of creation that enables us to correctly describe today's challenges in dealing with the gift of creation. Pope Francis comes back directly or indirectly to these pages in his own texts several times. So it makes sense to reproduce the most important passages from St Ignatius' *SE* which are relevant to the theology of creation.

> This is to recall to mind the blessings of creation and redemption, and the special favours I have received. I will ponder with great affection how much God our Lord has done for me, and how much He has given me of what He possesses, and finally, how much, as far as He can, the same Lord desires to give Himself to me according to His divine decrees …
>
> This is to reflect how God dwells in creatures: in the elements giving them existence, in the plants giving them life, in the animals conferring upon them sensation, in man bestowing understanding. So He dwells in me and gives me being, life, sensation, intelligence; and makes a temple of me, since I am created in the likeness and image of the Divine Majesty …
>
> This is to consider how God works and labours for me in all creatures upon the face of the earth, that is, He conducts Himself as one who labours. Thus, in the heavens, the elements, the

plants, the fruits, the cattle, etc., He gives being, conserves them, confers life and sensation, etc. ... This is to consider all blessings and gifts as descending from above. Thus, my limited power comes from the supreme and infinite power above, and so, too, justice, goodness, mercy, etc., descend from above as the rays of light descend from the sun, and as the waters flow from their fountains, etc. ...[2]

It is surprising how Ignatius depicts *God's dwelling amidst his creatures* and especially (though not exclusively) among human beings: given Ignatius' understanding of creation, God works on what constitutes their dignity so that they can realize it fully and develop who they are. He 'seeks' to make them express what they are through his gift. He specifically makes humankind his dwelling place, his *temple*, where his power, justice, kindness, friendship, compassion and mercy are to be found in the world and at work in the world. The powers that God gave human beings – freedom, memory, reason, will, all they have and possess[3] – are to be given back to the One who dwells in this temple, placed at his disposal, so that he can make them his instruments to bring creation to the development that the Creator made possible within them.

What God has put into his creation and into what he works in it, is developed in the love which animates the Creator in his work and which he wants to share with

---

2 *SE*, nos 234-237.
3 Cf. *Ibidem*, no. 234, second paragraph.

people, so that they recognize the work of his creation as his loving 'work' and collaborate in it. Ignatius' theology of creation is located here in the context of his contemplation on the attainment of love. Human beings can perceive love as the innermost reality of all being, and they can let it take possession of them if they perceive God's loving work in and on creation and consider it in its beauty. Of course, 'love ought to manifest itself in deeds rather than in words'.[4] But when the love that comes from God is realized in human beings, then we can say that 'love consists in a mutual sharing of goods, for example, the lover gives and shares with the beloved what he possesses, or something of that which he has or is able to give; and vice versa, the beloved shares with the lover'.[5] It then speaks of man giving back to God – whom he loves above all – what he has received; but less explicitly it also says that God is the recipient of love, and there is at least the tendency to also say that God needs what is given back to him: until his love is realized in creation and it blossoms.

Fully in line with Ignatius' *SE*, the Encyclical *LS* speaks of God's indwelling in creation, actively creating and perfecting it, of his 'work' in and with creation, which

4   *Ibidem*, no. 230; quoted in *Amoris Laetitia (AL)*, no. 94.
5   *Ibidem*, no. 231; cf. The brief commentary on this passage by W LAMBERT, „*Die Liebe besteht im Mitteilen von beiden Seiten". Von der Herzmitte ignatianischer Spiritualität*, in: TH GERTLER-ST, CH KESSLER-W. LAMBERT (eds.), *Zur größeren Ehre Gottes. Ignatius von Loyola neu entdeckt für die Theologie der Gegenwart*, Herder, Freiburg – Basel – Wien 2006, 141–159). *AL* refers to this passage of the *SE* indirectly, but in a central place (no. 157), where the question is how people become a gift to one another in sexual love.

should challenge human beings to become his collaborators. God is 'intimately present to each being, without impinging on the autonomy of his creature' (*LS*, no. 80). Each time he creates anew the self-reality of creatures, limiting himself as it were, and giving creatures room to act themselves.[6] Thus the Creator wants to 'work with us'; he counts on our involvement: on the fact, that is, that we consider the contexts and that we accept the painful developments that confront us in the world as the 'pains of childbirth' of

6 The metaphor of God's self-limitation is widespread in current theology. It probably comes from Medieval Jewish mysticism, is found in Isaac Luria and taken up again, for example, by Jürgen Moltmann. It assumes a spatial logic of approach: God must, so to speak limit himself in order to make room for a creature to be *beside him*. If he were to maintain his omnipotence, then creatures would not have autonomous power to act. They would be 'covered' by God's self-power. Cardinal Walter Kasper formulates this idea with a logical follow-up: 'God is sovereign and omnipotent precisely so that he can withdraw completely.' (W KASPER, *Barmherzigkeit. Grundbegriff des Evangeliums – Schlüssel christlichen Lebens*, Herder, Freiburg – Basel – Wien ⁵2015, 95) In English translation as *Mercy, the Essence of the Gospel and the Key to Christian Life*, Paulist Press, 2015. If – according to the reasoning of *LS* – the Creator-creature relationship is understood according to a communicative logic, the metaphor of God's self-limitation does not always appear to be appropriate. After all, God does not limit himself, but realizes himself in his availability and capacity to create relationships, in that he calls on his creatures – especially human beings – to be autonomous partners, and calls on them to enter into their freedom, given that he has given himzself to them 'as far as He can' (*SE*, no. 234; cf. W LAMBERT, „*Sie Liebe besteht im Mitteilen von beiden Seiten*, cit., 146). Cf., a deeper approach: J WERBICK, *Gott verbindlich. Eine theologische Gotteslehre*, Herder, Freiburg – Basel – Wien 2007, 402–406 (Italian: *Un Dio coinvolgente. Dottrina teologica su Dio, Queriniana*, Brescia 2010, 417–421).

something higher and more perfect, challenging us to 'the act of cooperation with the Creator' (*LS*, no. 80).

This does not mean, of course, that God, being immanent to creation in this sense, is integrated into it as Creator. Rather, one would have to speak of a transcendence-immanence of the Creator: God's creative, graceful work in creation enables it to transcend itself and thus participate in God's transcendence. According to *LS*, the entire creation is 'shaped by open and intercommunicating systems' in which we can discern 'countless forms of relationship and participation.' And that leads to the idea that the whole of the universe is also 'open to God's transcendence, within which it develops' (*LS*, no. 79).

God, the Creator, is immanent to the created universe in such a way that it enables him to self-transcend in the manifold relationships and interactions that make up and connect its open subsystems. His *indwelling* challenges the subsystems to develop ways of sharing, in which more and more participation and inclusion are realized and the exclusion or separation of individual elements is overcome. People are collaborators of the Creator because they allow themselves to be seized in freedom and love by God's trans-immanence – by God's liberating and challenging indwelling – and they try to live in collaboration with him as a loving self-transcendence towards the fullness which the Creator has intended for creation. According to the Jesuit theologian and palaeontologist Pierre Teilhard de Chardin, 'the ultimate destiny of the universe is in the fullness of God, which has already been attained by the risen Christ, the measure of the maturity of all things' (*LS*, no. 83).

In this tradition, therefore, creation is not a reality outside God. God goes out of himself in it and with it; in it he communicates himself and his love. In *LS* it says: 'The entire material universe speaks of God's love, his boundless affection for us. Soil, water, mountains: everything is, as it were, a caress of God' (*LS*, no. 84). In everything, the Creator wants to show and let us feel his love, to inspire us to respond to and share in it. God's creative out-going gives the whole of creation an inner dynamic of self-transcendence which is consciously assisted by human beings and so should also benefit our fellow creatures. Thus, created realities must never be disposed of solely for human self-interest. Following the example of St Francis, it is forbidden 'to turn reality into an object simply to be used and controlled' (*LS*, no. 11). The greatness and beauty of creation intends to and must express the glory of the Creator and his tender care for humanity (cf. *LS*, no. 12). People protect and defend and give glory to the Creator when they regard created realities not only as resources to be exploited, but as realities in themselves in which they may rejoice, and whose beauty they are called to acknowledge, a beauty that goes beyond their immediate usefulness: 'By learning to see and appreciate beauty, we learn to reject self-interested pragmatism. If someone has not learned to stop and admire something beautiful, we should not be surprised if he or she treats everything as an object to be used and abused without scruple' (*LS*, no. 215, cf. no. 29).

Creation makes God recognizable as the giver of an intimately good gift, who 'not only has entrusted the world to us men and women' but also gave us the gift of our lives, a gift which, of course, 'must be defended from various forms of debasement.' On the basis of 'God's original gift of all that is' such as our life, we are challenged to shape the world for the benefit of all – our fellow human beings, those who come after us, as well as all other creatures – so that everything that God wanted to give and share in creation will benefit (cf. *LS* no. 5). To regard creation as the gift of God is to honour the giver of this good gift by assuming joint responsibility to ensure this gift is and continues to be good.

Chapter 3
GOD'S GIFT — GOD'S CHALLENGE

According to *Laudato Si'* (*LS*), creation makes us aware of God's 'loving plan', so that people will allow themselves to be involved in cooperating in its realization. God counts on human beings for this plan of his. Yes, he relies on people and obviously takes a tremendous risk. Will people actually allow themselves to be collaborators in God's love, with his work in and with creation? Biblical faith in creation is clear about it: 'The Creator does not abandon us; he never forsakes his loving plan or repents of having created us' (*LS*, no. 13).

This belief is challenged by catastrophic experiences in nature and history that make many people doubt whether there actually is a 'loving plan' in creation, a love that gives them creation as a gift in their own lives for them to rejoice in and so they may grow in the love that this gift bears witness to. We are forced to agree that people mistreat and ruin God's gift, exploit it and ruthlessly grab whatever they can get. One may wonder why people are given so much power to do wrong. Is that the inevitable price to pay for their power to do good? If that were the case, from a human perspective (it is enough to consider the catastrophes of the 20th and even the 21st centuries), would not the Creator have taken an irresponsibly high risk?

But is it permissible to even ask that? Not only critics of religion in the 19th and 20th centuries have asked as much.

The victims of the 'death factory' at Auschwitz, survivors and witnesses, their contemporaries and later generations born after the world wars, have likewise asked the question. Christians felt not only challenged from outside, but they also doubted in their hearts, since 'it looks as if the Blessed Lord had created the world for the benefit of the devil! It would have been so much better not to have made it at all.'[1] In opposition to the traditional doctrine of Christian belief, Schopenhauer has sarcastically exaggerated what Jewish-born writer Elias Canetti recorded in his notes about his deep existential concern for the 20th century: 'The idea that life has been given to someone seems monstrous to me.'[2]

The fact that people can make the earth a hell for their fellow human beings is not just the experience of the 20th century. The fact that they are also involved in leaving those who come after them an earth in which the basic elements of life have deteriorated is not only a threat for people today, but is indeed the occasion for which the Encyclical *Laudato Si'* was written. However, people have always been plagued by natural disasters, which makes them wonder how it can be that the good gift of creation is associated with so much suffering and causes so much despair among the people who are at the mercy of such disasters.

Theology has no answers to cope with the gravity of these questions and which would eliminate the challenge

---

1 A SCHOPENHAUER, *Parerga und Paralipomena II, Sämtliche Werke*, W. FREIHERR VON LÖHNEYSEN (ed.), Taschenbuchausgabe Suhrkamp, Frankfurt a. M. 1986, Vol. V, 431.

2 E CANETTI, *Die Provinz des Menschen. Aufzeichnungen 1942–1972*, Hanser, München 1973, 309.

involved. These questions were summarized in a neologism, *theodicy*, by German philosopher Gottfried Wilhelm Leibniz.[3] The question of theodicy forms, as it were, the dark background inevitably involved in any biblical and Christian discourse about creation. With this background, one must at least explain why, in the face of moral evil and painful experiences in creation – in theological language, the *malum morale*, for which human beings bear responsibility, and the *malum physicum*, tied to the natural processes that occur in the world – the *possibility* remains open for faith to speak of a loving creator God whose creation is a good gift to people, who bears witness to his love and wants to communicate it.

The question of the *malum physicum* deals with the pre-given nature of physical evil, which seems to immediately contradict the idea of creation as a good gift. Attempts have also been made to link the physical evil preceding human action to a *malum morale* which would rightly punish human beings through the *malum physicum* – bodily death, natural disasters and lack of life of any kind; Augustine saw this and blamed it on original sin.[4] It is hard to maintain this view, given that the Church's teaching today on original sin has again become significant and the object of reflection.

---

3 Cf. GW Leibniz, *Die Theodizee. Von der Güte Gottes, der Freiheit des Menschen und dem Ursprung des Übels*, Philosophische Schriften, H Herring (ed.), Vol. II, Wissenschaftliche Buchgesellschaft, Darmstadt 1985. [This work *Theodicy*, is available in English online through Project Gutenberg].

4 Cf. his succinct statement: "The noun 'evil' is used in a double sense: what man does and what man suffers; one refers to sin, the other to punishment for sin" (Augustine, *Contra Adamantium* 26, *Patrologia Latina* 42, 169).

Currently, another approach is opening up to the mystery of moral and physical evil, by which humanity is already determined before the world and the self can determine human action, in this sense constituting the *situation* of human freedom.

The universe is a work in progress, a process of self-development and differentiation which human observations and theoretical constructions can survey 'to some extent', or can extrapolate more or less speculatively from what is observable, and then, if possible, reconnect with the corresponding data coming from observation. Using evolutionary modelling, people can statistically understand the emergence of extremely incredible interactions that ultimately determine the formation and evolution of the Milky Way, our solar system, and the evolution of life on our planet. These relationships are so complex and so incalculable for human research that at least the assertion critical of theodicy – that a benevolent God could have carried out the development of human beings in another way that would not have exposed them to infinite suffering and death on earth – cannot be considered as justifiable. The traditional reference to the example of the *malum physicum* of earthquakes and climatic catastrophes which affect so many innocent children, leads to contexts of the history of earth and climate today that make a less painful alternative seem hardly conceivable.

A theology of creation formulated in detailed fashion and in conversation with the empirical sciences would be able to speak of God, of course, as the origin of all being and of creation as the work of his good will. But it would understand creation in the sense we have outlined, as a work in progress which is realized according to internal natural laws, meaning that no other *realizable* ways can be devised. This leads us to suggest that God's work of creation follows laws that even he could not arbitrarily vary. This hypothesis goes against God's creative omnipotence only if we understand omnipotence as the power to want and to realize everything possible. This is not – as will be shown – a reasonable understanding of omnipotence. For God too, only what is *possible in itself* is possible for him, not just because he wants it. If, in the case of his creation, he was concerned with freely calling into existence those who would co-operate with his love – 'co-lovers'[5], this intention of creation may have bound him to the inner laws of a process, meaning that even for him there were not and still are not alternatives capable of producing less suffering.

This consideration does not answer theodicy's question about the *malum physicum*, but – in view of what we know today – it can merely be held open as a question. There are no indisputable arguments which compel believers to exclude a loving God as creator of the universe. Likewise, *LS's* central statement of faith, according to which God has created 'a world in need of development,' and that 'God in some way sought to limit himself in such a way that many of the things we think of as evils, dangers or sources of suffering, are in reality part of the pains of childbirth which he uses

---

5 DUNS SCOTUS: "God wants co-lovers" ("Deus vult condiligentes") (*Opus Oxoniense* III d. 32 q. 1 no. 6).

to draw us into the act of cooperation with the Creator' (*LS*, no. 80). From a belief perspective, the world is God's challenge to people to use and develop all their human potential to help make God's good will more and more a reality. To be a human being means not only to become the co-subject of the good and the beautiful that is possible in this world, but also to take on joint responsibility for the future of this world. The dignity of the human being lies precisely in the fact that we not only suffer and experience the world as it develops and the evolution of what is possible in the world, but in the fact that we are required to share in making them a reality and deciding *how* they will become a reality. God's work and 'effort' in the world's development (Ignatius of Loyola) seek to be and must be supported and taken up by people. This takes place through participation in the dynamics of the *creatio continua*, or ongoing creation, which is bound to the laws of evolutionary differentiation. The Creator 'invests' himself in this, and lets his good will toward his creatures be known.

Pope Francis' *Ignatian tradition* regarding creation places greater panentheistic emphasis on it than does the 'mainstream' Christian doctrine of creation. In this, it appears closer to current thinking than does a conception of creation which suggests a handiwork carried on from outside. God goes 'beyond himself' – metaphorically speaking – in his creative activity. He lives and works in his creation. But he is not identical with it. This is where the line is drawn with pantheism. God's *omnipotence* is realized in the very fact that he communicates his own autonomy and independence to the other and, as far as human beings are concerned, his freedom (cf. *LS*, no. 80).[6] Only with difficulty has this idea been established and formulated in the theology and philosophy of the West, and has found final if still groping expression only with Søren Kierkegaard. The relevant note is quoted here in context:

> The greatest good, after all, that can be done for a being, greater than anything else that one can do for it, is to make it free. In order to do just that, omnipotence is required. this seems strange, since it is precisely omnipotence that supposedly would make it [a being] dependent. But if one will reflect on omnipotence, one will see that it also must contain the unique qualification of being able to withdraw itself again in a manifestation of omnipotence in such a way that precisely for this reason that which has been originated through omnipotence can be independent ... Only omnipotence can withdraw itself at the same time it gives itself away, and this relationship is the very independence of the receiver. God's omnipotence is therefore his goodness. For goodness is to give oneself away completely, but in such a way that by omnipotently taking oneself back, one makes the recipient independent; only omnipotence can make [a being] independent, can form from nothing something that has its continuity in itself through the continuous withdrawing of omnipotence. Omnipotence is not ensconced

---

6 The Encyclical makes reference to *Gaudium et Spes*, no. 36, where it speaks of the 'autonomy of earthly affairs'.

> in a relationship to another, for there is no other to which it is comparable – no, it can give without giving up the least of its power, that is, it can make [a being] independent. It is incomprehensible that omnipotence is not only able to create the most impressive of all things – the whole visible world – but is able to create the most fragile of things – a being independent of that very omnipotence ... Creation out of nothing is once again the Almighty's expression for being able to make [a being] independent.[7]

Kierkegaard does not think of the human being's freedom as original in itself, but as created by God. The experience of the *personal presence* of God in the gift of my life, my world, gives me the opportunity to respond to this challenging presence of God, to open myself to it, to let me be enraptured by its beauty, to make room for it in me and in the world, to become an 'I' in it and beginning from it[8] – or, and this is difficult to understand, to deny itself. It

---

7 S Kierkegaard, *Reflexionen über Christentum und Naturwissenschaft*, in *Gesammelte Werke*, E Hirsch und H Gerdes (eds.), 17. Abteilung, Gütersloher Verlagshaus, Gütersloh 1983, 124 ff.

8 Thus, the text quoted above is to be read in conjunction with Kierkegaard's theory of the self, for example, in his *Sickness Unto Death* where the overcoming of despair and thus the possibility of the self – a relationship that is that could relate to itself without contradicting itself – are taken for granted in that "the self is transparently grounded in the power which it has posited" (*Die Krankheit zum Tode*, Gesammelte Werke, 24. und 25. Abteilung, Gütersloher Verlagshaus, Gütersloh 1992, 10). The divine power of the Creator on which the self is based sets the self free, as it allows it to realize itself as this relationship that relates to itself –

is a personal presence that calls on human beings, giving them the opportunity to discover in this call that as the addressees of this call, they can be (co-) subjects of their life and their world, and in this sense can respond to the call: in this presence there is the omnipotent relational power of God's love, his inexhaustible availability to the relationship in which he wants to be there with and for human beings.⁹ With regard to creation as a whole, it 'not only manifests God but is also a locus of his presence. The Spirit of life dwells in every living creature and calls us to enter into relationship with him' (*LS*, no. 88).¹⁰ Human beings, however, are called to perceive God's presence, his availability for relationship with them and the world, and to respond to and bear witness to a life of self-transcendence in an existence spent on behalf of their fellow human beings.

The fact that human beings deny this calling to a terrifying degree, and sabotage the *creatio continua* instead of collaborating with it, is theodicy's challenge where the *malum morale* is concerned. Human beings abuse the power of being which is imparted to them and aroused by God's self-communication in them, in order to raise themselves to the point of being god over others (Gen 3:4) and profit

and hence never to fail because the relation between infinity and finitude cannot come about of its own accord.

9 Kierkegaard's text follows, at least implicitly, the logic of the metaphor of the omnipotent Creator who limits himself. This logic does not mean that the Creator, in his personal presence in creation, goes beyond himself, so for my part I follow a metaphorical logic; cf. The previous chapter, note no. 6.

10 Quoted by the NATIONAL CONFERENCE OF BISHOPS OF BRAZIL, *A Igreja e a questão ecológica* (1992), nn. 53–54.

from their goodness. Does this abuse of freedom and power also belong to the 'pains of childbirth' of a creation in the process of evolutionary self-development? Did God then 'have to' grant the possibility of selfishly abusing creation so that people could become his partners in the process of ongoing creation?

No argument of theodicy will be convincing enough to be able to positively 'justify' God. This also applies in view of the *malum morale*. To some extent, however, from the argumentative point of view, one can perhaps share the fact that, according to our current state of knowledge, the polarization between aggressive self-affirmation and self-transcendence, which is instead the basis of a relationship, and which makes cooperation and the experience of the added value of communion possible beyond pure self-reference, is part of the evolution of human life. The fact that this tension is all too often resolved in favour of the pole of aggressive self-assertion and that self-affirmation is sought in denying others, even by resorting to violence, is a feature of the historical experience of humanity. It is the dark side of the finite human capacity for relationship that God himself is involved in and to which, in his Christ, he exposes his presence in the world. In Christ, in the divine revelations of religions, and especially in the chosen people of Israel, God tries to get people to dare to transcend themselves through love and thus be at the service of creation.[11] In a certain sense

11 This aspect of the relationship between God and humanity was developed in the twentieth century by the *theology of process* – which is linked to Alfred N. Whitehead's *philosophy of process* – which tries to understand how the Creator is involved

he 'repairs' human catastrophes, but not 'from the outside'; he intervenes by demanding that human beings cooperate in creation – fulfil their justice toward creation. Would he have had other, less 'risky' opportunities to win over people as contributors to his creation? That must remain an open question for theology. Ultimately, in theology, it can only be a question of tracing the humanly comprehensible meaning of God's ways with people and comprehending with the best possible arguments what it means for God and human beings that God wants to be so intimately close to them.

In this sense, looking ahead, the following can be said: God's immanence in creation is to be thought of as the presence in creation which personally challenges humanity – challenges it to be self-transcendent. The Christian theology of creation has not always kept in mind or thought rigorously about this contemporaneous 'suprapersonal' (Christological-pneumatic) dynamic of God's immanence in creation and his personal-communicative presence. But it is precisely in the Ignatian tradition of the Jesuits that this task has been taken up again and again. *LS*, no. 83 in particular speaks

---

in creation and makes himself present in it, not determining it 'from outside', but by challenging it with his pleading, enticing approach to its sense of creation. Cf. Summary in CHR LINK, *Schöpfung. Schöpfungstheologische Herausforderungen des 20. Jahrhunderts* (Handbuch Systematischer Theologie, Bd. 7/2), Gütersloher Verlagshaus, Gütersloh 1991, 428–446 and J ENXING, *Gott im Werden. Die Prozesstheologie Charles Hartshornes*, Pustet, Regensburg 2013. It remains to be understood how exactly the in-being [*In-Sein*] of God in his creation and his personal attitude toward it [*Gegenüber*] can be related to each other, and also how one can speak of a 'becoming' of God.

of *Pierre Teilhard de Chardin* and his cosmic-pneumatic Christology in an important context. The objection has often be raised against *Teilhard* that he too directly connects God's immanence in creation with the dynamic of the self-transcendence of evolution. This criticism can hardly apply to *Karl Rahner*, who elaborates on the question dealt with here:

> The self-communication of God, in which God communicates himself as the absolute Transcendent, is the most immanent factor in the creature. The fact that he gives it a proper being, the "immanence of being" in this sense, is both the presupposition and consequence of the still more radical immanence of the transcendence of God in the spiritual creature ... Models constructed on the "internal-external" difference fail here: the persistence of this radically different God in communicating himself is the most internal [he is present to himself], but it is also the very possibility of the immanence of what is most external [in him].[12]

The innermost dynamic of the divine immanence in creation is at the same time the most external challenge to participation in that movement of self-transcendence in which God communicates himself to people as love so that they may participate in it and find their fullness in it. Thus

---

12 K RAHNER, *Immanente und transzendente Vollendung der Welt*, in DERS., *Schriften zur Theologie*, Vol. VIII, Benziger, Einsiedeln – Zürich – Köln 1967, 593–609, 601.

the inner-outer scheme is thus infiltrated here, maintaining the tension between a being-within of God in all things – understood in a panentheistic sense and always difficult to comprehend – and his personal being-there-before [*Gegenüber*].¹³ The Biblical-Christian idea of both God and creation prevents our choosing one at the expense of the other; and it refers to the theology of the Trinity, in which this cohesion in the coexistence of the three divine persons finds its theological basis.

This conceptual reference system appears to be as undeniable in contemporary theology – and as the cited texts indicate, it is also normative for Pope Francis – as the concepts are different that seek to consistently ponder God's immanence in creation and God's transcendence in its regard in personal confrontation with humanity. This is unproblematic as long as one can define a common theological starting point beyond all the differences in schools of thought.¹⁴

---

13   Philosopher Peter Strasser speaks in this sense of the "God who is personal and at the same time is everything"; P Strasser, *Der Gott aller Menschen. Eine philosophische Grenzüberschreitung*, Styria, Graz – Wien – Köln 2002, 191.

14   This basic understanding also underlies my controversy with Klaus Müller's monistic-inspired concept. Cf. J Werbick, *Gott verbindlich*, 632–638 (*Un Dio coinvolgente (A God who involves)*, 669–676); K Müller, *Streit um Gott. Politik. Poetik und Philosophie im Ringen um das wahre Gottesbild*, Pustet, Regensburg 2006.

Chapter 4
JUSTICE-AS-GIFT

God 'goes out of himself'. He communicates himself, so that even his creation challenges human beings and 'entices' them to share in his love in which he goes out of himself. Even despite all the suffering and cruelty that it permeates as a reality of nature, Creation is his gift. People accept this when they perceive God's creative intention and thus share in God's 'work' in and with creation, and, as far as is possible for them, develop its potential. This is not to be cynical about the biblical belief in God. To the contrary, this belief puts its trust in the fact that collaboration in God's creation is not in vain, but rather enters into the perfecting of creation guaranteed by God.

The more clearly believers perceive the goodness and beauty of creation, the more strongly they realize the common obligation to serve this goodness and beauty God has given to creation; and the clearer the challenge is for them to testify in word and deed to the palpable and visible goodness of God in creation. The goodness and beauty of creation (cf. the Hebrew word *tov* in Gen 1:1-2,4) must not therefore be selfishly appropriated and made subject to my disposal, so that it would only be good for me. The one who has given the gift for everyone, wants to be honoured in it. Individuals, therefore, cannot claim to have any 'absolute possession' in its regard. For biblical Israel, the gift of the earth is each person's livelihood and everyone is subject to the proviso that what is given to a person by God may not be permanently taken away from them. 'The land shall not be sold in perpetuity, for the land is mine; for you are strangers and sojourners with me' (Lev 25:23; *Laudato Si'*, no, 67, *LS*). This 'reservation of ownership' is not intended to arbitrarily restrict the enjoyment of creation, but to enforce the fact that the gift of creation must be shared justly so that everyone participates in it. The jubilee year would ensure that the greed of the powerful is limited: every fifty years, the original property relationships are to be restored, according to which everyone in Israel can live on the land assigned to him (cf. Lev 25:8-12; *LS* no. 711).[1] And other creatures too should be granted their due habitat. They must not be endlessly exploited, but have 'a value of their own in God's eyes' (cf. *LS*, nos 68-69 with reference to Deut 22:4.6 or Ex 23:12). In this sense, the creation as a whole is to be accorded '*the priority of being over that of being useful*' (*LS*, no. 69).[2]

The creation theology of *LS* is based on a concept of justice that is more biblical and more contemporary than the ideals of a formal justice in the sense of 'each to his own'. It is more contemporary because it sees the being

---

1   In exegetical research it is disputed whether such jubilee years actually existed or whether this tradition is more likely to keep alive the memory of God's justice against an already widespread landlordism.

2   Quote taken from the SECRETARIAT OF THE GERMAN EPISCOPAL CONFERENCE (ed.) *Zukunft der Schöpfung – Zukunft der Menschheit. Erklärung der Deutschen Bischofskonferenz zu Fragen der Umwelt und der Energieversorgung* (Die deutschen Bischöfe Nr. 28), Bonn 1980, II. 2.

of creatures within a comprehensive network of creation in which something can exist for others and yet not lose its own value. In such a network, where we exist for one another, human beings are called to perceive the goodness of God the Creator who gives, and to protect it from being torn apart because people are too selfish.[3] As far as they can, human beings are obliged to involve others in being part of the positive relationships of interaction that sustain and develop this network. They are obliged to make accessible and keep as such, the opportunities for life that they can access when they are allowed to participate in this network of creation and life. Whoever arbitrarily or in their own self-interest excludes human beings, but also other creatures, from this being-there-for each other, sabotages the goodness and beauty of creation. People of this kind act in a *fundamentally unjust way* and contribute to the sin that tears apart the goodness of creation. Anyone who makes room for sin concretely denies the right of other creatures to exist, because they are despising the relationships of existence and life in which such a right has its value.

In a biblical sense, justice fundamentally means justice in existence and life. It starts with the Creator, who created it and

---

3   In *LS*, no. 220, Pope Francis says that believers 'do not look at the world from without but from within, conscious of the bonds with which the Father has linked us to all beings.' The 'splendid universal communion' we form with 'the rest of creatures' is fulfilled in positive interactions between the creatures he spoke of earlier, in which human beings are called to develop their 'individual God-given capacities.'

assigned it to creatures, especially human beings.[4] YHWH, the benevolent and life-loving God of Israel, repeatedly intercedes for them, according to biblical testimonies, whenever they are disregarded by the powerful or at least not adequately protected. What has been given and is still being given to human beings by God, when he incorporates them into the good interrelationships of creation, must not be taken away from them or denied by the powerful and the malicious. Thus, YHWH gives his people the *Torah*, which seeks to reveal and make binding on them just how his justice is to be realized among people and for Israel: or in other words how, with regard to the work of creation, it is incumbent on every living being and especially human beings to support and nourish life before and with God. The *Torah* draws attention to what is worthy and demanding of protection, to what demands justice, sharing what God has given (cf. *LS*, no. 71), and seeing that no one is deprived of what he or she needs to be able to live as God's creature and lead a decent human life.

From a biblical point of view, God himself is the original and enduring Just being who proves his justice *by giving it*. It is his good gift 'that must make life with God and other human beings possible for man. Thus [the *Torah*] is a directive to life, and [it] gives a really comprehensive *jioe*

---

4 According to conventional wisdom, justice must be safeguarded and restored in terms of people. Biblically, the view is widened to include other creatures, even though - and this applies to the present day – it is not sufficiently clear to what extent or to what degree or with what restrictions one can speak of "subjects" here to whom justice should be shown.

di vivre.⁵ Just conditions prevail where people are trustingly involved in the good relationships of creation and can *rely* on the fact that their legitimate desire for the essentials and life-promoting factors is properly taken into account: that is, the gift of life must not appear to them to be a serious imposition because it holds them back from what should constitute a 'good life.'⁶ Injustices are relationships that hinder God's bringing in [*hereinholen*]⁷ justice and unjustifiably exclude people: from participation in the goods and opportunities for life with which they could realize themselves; from co-determining and shaping the life contexts in which they lead their lives. Those who are left out must experience being cut off from one or other aspect of life. The justice which comes from God and should be for the benefit of human beings is not realized in their regard: God's justice is inclusive, integrating, guarantees participation, canvasses [*hereinholen*] on behalf of life, is at the service of life, corresponding to the gift of the Creator and which should be guaranteed for all.

From a biblical point of view, justice is realized when the relationships which make possible or generate life and

---

5   G Obst – F Crüsemann, *Müssen sich Christinnen und Christen an das Gesetz des Alten Testaments halten?*, in F Crüsemann – U Theismann (eds.), *Ich glaube an den Gott Israels. Fragen und Antworten zu einem Thema, das im christlichen Glaubensbekenntnis fehlt*, Gütersloher Verlagshaus, Gütersloh 1993, 11–118, 115. Cf. also J. Werbick, *Gnade* (Grundwissen der Theologie), Schöningh, Paderborn 2013, 20f.

6   Cf. Bertolt Brecht's poem 'Bitten der Kinder' (Children's Prayers) with its central request that "Life should not be a punishment"; B Brecht, *Gesammelte Gedichte*, Suhrkamp, Frankfurt a. M. 1976, 995.

7   The verb literally means "go and bring in" or "canvass for"

vitality *are accessible and are rendered accessible.* The criterion which governs such relationships in this case is not primarily concerned with formal equivalence in the sense of 'to each his own',[8] but is understood by starting from what serves this relationship: justice is at the service of safeguarding vital relationships in which each individual finds what is 'necessary' and can develop; relationships, therefore, in which the *shalom* guaranteed by God is the governing factor. Only on this basis and for its sake does the criterion which formally governs the relationship have its truly essential meaning. Accessibility means one can share in a gift in which all recipients are to share to an appropriate degree: to the extent, that is, that they allow themselves to be served by this gift in such a way that it can be fruitful and beneficial for as many people as possible. God is just because he makes life accessible and thus makes himself accessible so that life can be good and can be had in abundance. People should be involved in this primordial active justice – this justice-as-gift. This is conferred on Israel through the gracious gift of *Torah*. It is shared with Christians in the incarnate *Logos* who wants to lead them incumbent on each person. Primarily, in the sense of participative justice, it consists in the right way of receiving, protecting and sharing what is received. It fundamental movement is the receiving and offering of participation; any denial of participation is fundamental injustice.

[8] The classic formulation of this principle is found in DOMITIUS ULPIANUS, *Corpus Iuris Civilis*, Digesten 1,1,10 ('Justice is the constant and perpetual willingness to attribute to each what is his right' [*Iustitia est constans et perpetua voluntas ius suum cuique tribuendi*]); cf. CICERO, *De legibus* 1,6,19.

If this momentous shift in the thinking and practice of justice is realized, one gains the *theo*-logical perspective in which the often critically perceived provocation of the *Concluding Document of the Episcopal Conference of Aparecida* and then of the Apostolic Exhortation *Evangelii Gaudium* (*EG*) becomes an exemplary testimony of Christian faith. Human justice demands that the excluded share in, and are brought into [*hereinholen*] the economy, society *and Church*. Exclusion, refusal of participation, are in principle contrary to creation. When, for whatever reason, it is considered necessary and imposed, it would need to be legitimized most rigorously. All strategies of legitimization, from this point of view, are open to the suspicion (not easily removed) of being ideological bias on the part of corresponding power interests. What is self-evident from a strictly theological point of view leads to participation that is just in terms of humanity and creation. What is not completely or absolutely self-evident must not only have good reasons for itself, but must be able to demonstrate that it is at the service of what is theologically self-evident, if it is to be done inn a lawful manner.

Unacceptable, because fundamentally contrary to creation, are 'the living conditions of many of those who are abandoned, excluded, and ignored in their poverty and pain.' They contradict the 'project of the Father and challenge believers to greater commitment to the culture of life.' Believers are exhorted to commit themselves to overcoming 'grave social inequalities and the enormous differences in access to goods' (*Aparecida*, no. 358). Believers are to support the option for the poor and the excluded, and be there with active solidarity in 'the new realities of exclusion and marginalization in which the more vulnerable groups live, where life is most in jeopardy.' The Latin American Episcopal Conference pays particular attention to:

> the new excluded: migrants, victims of violence, displaced people and refugees, victims of human trafficking and kidnappings, the disappeared, people sick with HIV and endemic diseases, drug addicts, adults, boys and girls who are victims of prostitution, pornography and violence or of child labour, abused women, victims of exclusion and traffic for sexual exploitation, differently-abled people, large groups of unemployed men and women, those excluded by technological illiteracy, street people in large cities, the indigenous and Afro-Americans, landless peasants and miners (*Aparecida*, no. 402).

All these kinds of people remain outside from many points of view, if indeed they are not even alienated from the networks and processes in which creation continues – the *creatio continua* – and wants to lead people to a creative development of life. Christians obey the 'basic law of reality' according to which life finds its fulfilment only through its incorporation into a comprehensive communio of creation and life, 'in fraternal and just communion.' They can 'conceive of an offer of life in Christ' only by entering into a 'dynamism toward integral liberation, humanization, reconciliation, and involvement in society' (*Aparecida*, no. 359). This dynamism by which they brought into [*hereinholen*] and integrated within society reflects the dynamism of creation in which God's love allows people to share in God's own creative presence and leads them to the fullness of life.

Nevertheless – according to *EG* – the entire economic system is built on exclusion and marginalization which are contrary to creation. Thus the Apostolic Exhortation says a clear

> 'No to an economy of exclusion,' ... Such an economy kills. How can it be that it is not a news item when an elderly homeless person dies of exposure, but it is news when the stock market loses two points? This is a case of exclusion. Can we continue to stand by when food is thrown away while people are starving? This is a case of inequality. Today everything comes under the laws of competition and the survival of the fittest, where the powerful feed upon the powerless. As a consequence, masses of people find themselves excluded and marginalized: without work, without possibilities, without any means of escape. Human beings are themselves considered consumer goods to be used and then discarded ... It is no longer simply about exploitation and oppression, but something new. Exclusion ultimately has to do with what it means to be a part of the society in which we live; those excluded are no longer society's underside or its fringes or its disenfranchised – they are no longer even a part of it. The excluded are not the

'exploited' but the outcast, the 'leftovers' (*EG*, no. 53).

Those outside are no longer even perceived. A lifestyle has developed that does not want to be disturbed by the excluded, a 'globalization of indifference' to everything that happens and suffers 'outside' (*EG*, no. 54).

In this case a power contrary to creation is spreading, which is called structural evil and about which *EG* says: 'Just as goodness tends to spread, the toleration of evil, which is injustice, tends to expand its baneful influence and quietly to undermine any political and social system, no matter how solid it may appear. If every action has its consequences, an evil embedded in the structures of a society has a constant potential for disintegration and death. It is evil crystallized in unjust social structures, which cannot be the basis of hope for a better future' (*EG*, no. 59).

Believers and the Churches are called upon to oppose this anti-culture of exclusion and disintegration so that creation can have a future. They are meant to testify to the gesture of creational inclusion which is the gesture of the Creator himself, and with which he wishes to bring creatures in [*hereinholen*], human beings especially, to the process of the development of creation, letting them share in himself. *EG* appeals to the Churches, firstly to the Catholic Church, to leave the mindset of exclusion behind. They are entrusted with the gospel and the grace Jesus Christ gave them along the way to save human beings from what the evil one would have as their destiny. The Church of Jesus Christ must always be 'the house of the Father, with doors always wide open,' never closed to the needs and abandonment of the excluded, who have often been excluded even by her (cf. *EG*, nos 46-47). 'The word of God constantly shows us how God challenges those who believe in him "to go forth",' infecting them with the joy of the Holy Spirit to make them 'go forth from [their] own comfort zone in order to reach all the "peripheries" in need of the light of the Gospel' (*EG*, no. 20).

'The drive to go forth and give, to go out from ourselves' (*EG*, no. 21) accepts God's own profound movement, his going out of himself in creation that brings [*hereinholen*] Jesus Christ into the midst of humanity. He went out to the marginalized in order to witness to them that God is for them. He invites us 'constantly to run the risk of a face-to-face encounter with others, with their physical presence which challenges us, with their pain and their pleas, with their joy which infects us in our close and continuous interaction' (*EG*, no. 88). Jesus Christ considers it his mission to go out of himself to be with the excluded, to be moved and touched by their plight, to bring the forsaken once more into the network which will benefit creation, into the 'flock of those who seek life among them and find it in the presence of God – in God's Lordship (cf. Lk 15:3-6). He wants to entrust all this to those who accept the path he has taken. Together with him they should 'boldly take the initiative, go out to others, seek those who have fallen away, stand at the crossroads and welcome the outcast. Such a community has an endless desire to show mercy, the fruit of its own experience of the power of the Father's infinite mercy. Let us try a little harder to take the first step and to become involved. Jesus washed the feet of his disciples. The Lord gets involved and he involves his own' (*EG*, no. 24).

God goes out of himself and is involved – in his Christ – in seeking out the lost, showing them mercy. He also wants the Church to be involved in this outgoing movement – of mercy – and to overcome its selfishness, leave ecclesiastical narcissism behind (cf. *EG*, nos 20-21). In this we touch on a leitmotif of Pope Francis' proclamation about God, a theme like no other, running through the way he exercises his ministry but also his theological choices: the mercy of God.

Chapter 5
GOD IS MERCIFUL

In our contemporary scene, the word 'mercy' evokes quite contrasting associations.[1] In legal and theological usage, along with 'grace', the word 'mercy' often takes on the meaning of a 'sovereign' suspension of justice in which 'grace prevails over law' to spare the guilty. In itself, the guilty should expect the punishment owed to them, but *mercy* is shown them, opening the 'door of grace'. In the Catholic Church, the age-old custom of the *Holy Year*, tied to the Old Testament tradition of the Jubilee Year, has been added to this understanding of the term, found in Pope Francis' Apostolic Letter at the conclusion of the Extraordinary Jubilee of Mercy, *Misericordia et Misera* (*MeM*), on 20 November 2016: the year of mercy is meant to serve the Church's proclamation of the practice of *forgiveness*. It is 'is the most visible sign of the Father's love, which Jesus

---

1   According to no. 2 of Pope John Paul II's Encyclical of 30 November 1980, *Dives in Misericordia*, 'The word and the concept of "mercy" seem to cause uneasiness in man' and this is attributed to 'the enormous development of science and technology, never before known in history' thanks to which 'it has become the master of the earth and has subdued and dominated it.' The Encyclical goes on to say: 'This dominion over the earth, sometimes understood in a one-sided and superficial way, seems to have no room for mercy.' So perhaps we need to look at how this desire for mercy is to be expressed today, in order not to be consigned without scruple to this lack of mercy.

sought to reveal by his entire life' (*MeM*, no. 2). Mercy, as the Church showed with particular effort during the Holy Year, is demonstrated by the fact that 'even if the inclination to sin remains, it is overcome by the love that makes it possible for [the woman taken in adultery] to look ahead and to live her life differently' (*MeM*, no. 1).[2]

Nevertheless, Pope Francis does not limit the meaning of this term to *mercy toward the perpetrators* – sinners. He also keeps *mercy to the victims* theologically in mind. So he pleads for a culture of mercy, which he contrasts, at least symbolically – for example, through 'works of mercy' – with the lack of mercy in our world and economic order.[3] When *MeM* encourages priests, in the context of the year of mercy 'to be *welcoming* to all', this applies especially when encountering those who seek forgiveness (*MeM*, no. 10). But he appeals also to their active solidarity, in that they must also take to heart the needs of these individuals. The year of mercy has taught the Church '"that God bends down to us" (Hos 11:4) so that we may imitate him in bending

---

2 The Church seeks to follow its Lord. His 'Mercy will always be greater than any sin, and no one can place limits on the love of God who is ever ready to forgive': Bull of indiction of the Extraordinary Jubilee of Mercy, *Misericordiae Vultus* (*MV*), 11 April 2015, no. 3.

3 Pope Francis describes the works of mercy as 'handcrafted' (*MeM*, no. 20), a mercy which, nevertheless – as he clarifies in *Evangelii Gaudium* (*EG*) – is not limited to bandaging wounds, but nor does it refrain from doing so. Here Pope Francis draws inspiration from W Kasper, *Misericordia. Concetto fondamentale del vangelo*, (Mercy as the Essence of the Gospel) where there is also pointed reference to a culture of mercy (cf. 268-303; 247-257 or, in its German original, 179-202; 164-171).

down to our brothers and sisters' (*MeM*, no. 16). Hosea, but also for example in Psalms, speaks of God's mercy in a more extended sense, not only in reference to sinners. 'He executes justice for the oppressed; he gives food to the hungry. The Lord sets the prisoners free; the Lord opens the eyes of the blind. The Lord lifts up those who are bowed down; the Lord loves the righteous. The Lord watches over the sojourners, he upholds the widow and the fatherless' (Ps 146:7-9).[4] Mercy does not leave the needy and sinners in the lurch. *MV* tells us: 'He feels responsible; that is, he desires our well-being and he wants to see us happy, full of joy, and peaceful. This is the path which the merciful love of Christians must also travel' (*MV*, no. 9). Everyone must pursue '*the way of charity*' and 'the road of mercy, on which we meet so many of our brothers and sisters who reach out for someone to take their hand and become a companion on the way' (*MeM*, no. 16).

To some people this might seem to be like *condescension*. It poses the problem that mercy assumes a power gap: those to whom mercy is shown find themselves in the helpless position of being 'the wretched' who must gratefully accept that someone bends down to them and offers a hand.[5] It is then noted that the gap in power between the less privileged, often also the wretched, and the 'more powerful',

---

4 Text cited in *MV*, no. 6.

5 Mercy then becomes 'insolence: insolence for those who practise it and for the those who receive it'; it is especially so for the latter, because in their misery they must recognize their dependence on the other's pity; cf. J Knop, *Gottes Barmherzigkeit denken. Herausforderung für die dogmatische Theologie*, in *Zeitschrift für katholische Theologie* 138 (2016), 398–412, 398 and 411.

can be bridged and overcome more creatively through *empowerment*, giving strength back to the weak and getting them to share effectively in society. Thus we come to a discussion about concepts. It is by no means an insignificant one, since in the end it needs to be part of the matter, and can help the Church and society to overcome shortcomings and fixations in understanding the words used. Therefore, discussion about the concept of mercy should be given its proper place in the context of discourse about God; in the confidence that the semantic value of this term can emerge in the context of other concepts, and thus be 'saved'.

Reservations concerning *simple* mercy in a democratic constitutional state will also stem from the fact that one feels better 'protected' in the context of legal relationships regulated by certain rights and duties, compared to somewhat feudal situations where one depends on the good favour of the powerful. The 'hardness of the law', even the ruthlessness of the marketplace, still seem more manageable than the unpredictable benevolence of rulers and their 'justice'. Undoubtedly this is a strongly appreciated gain in freedom which shapes and supports the citizen's self-awarenes today.[6] The state legal system respects citizens precisely by dealing

---

6 Nietzsche contrasts this with the faith Christians place in a merciful God. If – Nietzsche says – the ego has become *loathsome* through sin, how could we "allow and accept others to love him/her – be they God or men! It would be contrary to all decency to allow oneself to be loved and also know very well that one deserves only loathing" (F NIETZSCHE, Morgenröthe, Aphorismus 79, KSA 3, 78). (eds.). In English translation as *Daybreak: Thoughts on the Prejudices of Morality*, Cambridge University Press, 1997.

with them according to justice and not according to good grace apparently without motivation.[7] Grace should be involved when an individual case is difficult to classify and no other way can be found to deal with it.

To be dependent on grace and mercy before God is bound up with the idea – not easily tolerated in modern times – of having absolutely lost any rights in his regard, inasmuch as transgression against God goes beyond any relationship classifiable according to law, and in any case, God does not offer any possibility of exercising justice and hence saving man from eternal perdition. What horrendous crime has made human beings so despicable before God that all they can do is hope in his mercy? For many people, the awareness of being so abysmally and profoundly unworthy before God no longer makes sense. This probably accounts for the deep irritation felt by the modern citizen, connected with the idea of *mercy shown to the perpetrators (sinners)*: there is a problem with mercy that has its obscure basis in the depravity of the human race, a depravity that only God can overcome through his tireless and insuperable mercy.

And mercy shown *to victims*? Here too a contradiction is felt which gives rise to irritation. Do not victims have a

---

7 Thus Georg Wilhelm Friedrich Hegel can claim, regarding punishment, that "In so far as the punishment which this entails is seen as embodying the criminal's *own right*, the criminal is honoured as a rational being" (G. W. F. HEGEL, *Grundlinien der Philosophie des Rechts*, § 100, K MOLLENHAUER-K. M. MICHEL (eds.), *Werke in zwanzig Bänden*, Vol. 7, Suhrkamp, Frankfurt a. M. 1970, 191). In English as Hegel, GWF 1821/1991. *Elements of the Philosophy of Right*. Ed. A. Wood. Transl. by HB Nisbet. Cambridge: Cambridge University Press.

declared human right to be removed from their misery and returned to their human dignity? Should they be dependent on mercy instead of fighting for their rights and demanding them from us, or from those responsible for their misery? Are they even dependent on our pity instead of our active solidarity? Does that not make them prisoners of their role as victims? Friedrich Nietzsche has put this reply into the mouth of his 'prophet' Zarathustra: 'Verily, I like them not, the merciful ones, whose bliss is in their pity: too destitute are they of bashfulness.' They degrade others with their pity, instead of strengthening them; they do not love with great, pure love, because: 'All great love is above all its pity: for it seeketh—to create what is loved.' And that is precisely why it does not offer 'a resting-place for his suffering,' but 'a hard bed, however, a camp-bed,' a strong encouragement which forces him to grow.[8]

Are the compassionate, then, not lacking in shame for shaming others with their pity? Nietzsche's response to compassion [*Mitleid*] and mercy has become deeply ingrained in language. But this should not be too easily given into – especially bearing in mind the Bible. Nevertheless, there has also been an effort in theology to avoid terms like this that arouse so much suspicion. Johann Baptist Metz has spoken of compassion using precisely this English word, 'compassion', meaning to heed the testimony of those who suffer, which makes us uncomfortable and disturbs the

---

8 *Also sprach Zarathustra* II. Von den Mitleidigen, KSA 4, 113–116. (Nietzsche's works are readily available in English translation online).

conscience of civil society, and hence also its theology. The English term was used primarily in the political debate of the sixties and seventies in the United States – especially by John F. and Robert Kennedy – and by Willy Brandt in the public language of the former West Germany.[9] Brandt used the English word compassion for the first time when speaking at the Dortmunder Party Congress of the SPD in 1972: "The translation of compassion is not easy, but the correct translation is the willingness to sympathize, the ability to be merciful, to love others. Dear friends, I tell you, and I say it to the citizens of our people, have the courage for this kind of compassion! Have the courage of mercy! Give courage to your neighbour! Reflect on these values which are so often mistreated! Find the road that leads to yourselves!' This opened up an intense political and public debate in Germany about the politico-social dimension of mercy: to be merciful as a way of acting that recognizes the needy circumstances of others and aims at giving back the possibilities for participation in the community. Compassion and mercy are thus seen not as condescension or as mere emotional concern because of our closeness to other, but are understood as an impulse to act on behalf of greater 'justice in participation and in sharing one's abilities'.[10]

9 The term seems to have been suggested to the Chancellor of West Germany, Willy Brandt, by journalist Klaus Harprecht, the most important speech-writer for Willy Brandt from 1972 onwards.

10 Thus, for example– still in connection with Willy Brandt – in a policy paper for the *Christians in the SPD* Group entitlede, *Gerechtigkeit und Barmherzigkeit. Anstöße und Materialien für eine*

Metz explores the use of this term in a crucial way in his theological intervention. In fact he speaks of a 'mysticism of *compassion*', saying that it is a 'mysticism of open eyes', a 'mysticism of the passion of God as compassion'.[11]

It brings a fundamental change of perspective in the following of Christ where one is affected by perceiving the others' suffering. In communion of spirit and faith with the Jewish philosopher Emmanuel Lévinas, Metz says: 'The authority of God [is manifested] in the authority of the those who suffer.' In reference to Mt 25:31-47 Metz says, 'they are not considered as an earthly equivalent of God's nearness, but as the earthly manifestation of it.'[12] In them, God wants to come near with his provocative word and suggest to people that they be challenged to heed the cry of the suffering[13] and the sight of their distress; that they let

zukunftsfähige sozialdemokratische Sozialpolitik, January 2012 (on the Internet: www.akc-bw.de/gerechtigkeitundbarmherzigkeit, visited on 12 April 2017).

11   Cf JB METZ, *Mit der Autorität der Leidenden. Compassion – Vorschlag zu einem Weltprogramm des Christentums*, in *Süddeutsche Zeitung* No. 296 from 24./25./26. December 1997, Cultural insert, p. 1; ID., In collaboration with *Johann Reikerstorfer, Memoria passionis. Ein provozierendes Gedächtnis in pluralistischer Gesellschaft*, Herder, Freiburg-Basel-Wien 2006, 105–107 and 166ff. The metaphor of 'mysticism of open eyes' is semantically in contrast to the literal meaning of the root *myo* (closed, eyes closed) from which the understanding of the term 'mysticism' is traditionally derived.

12   *JB METZ, Memoria passionis, 106; cf. E LÉVINAS, Die Spur des Anderen, dt. Alber, Freiburg-München 1992, 220–230.*

13   Cf. JB METZ, *Memoria passionis*, 8–11, where Metz picks up the metaphor of the "stones crying out" from Nelly Sachs (N. SACHS, *Landschaft aus Schreien. Ausgewählte Gedichte*, Aufbau, Weimar 1966).

themselves be led by their authority into the authority of the word of God and be recalled to their responsibility for those who suffer. With Hans Jonas, the slogan 'Look and you will know!' should be regarded as a categorical imperative of compassion.[14] This can be completed by saying: 'Open your eyes and you will know to what and why you are called!'

The mysticism of open eyes (and open ears) shares in God's perception and it is a call to duty: so that people no longer pretend not to see and hear what must be seen and heard, and so that it will no longer continue. At the same time this mysticism is a lament about why it still persists, why we continue to call out *'Maranatha'* – Come, Lord Jesus!, and why the unbearable still has to be endured. For believers, this lament would mean being called to the 'following of *compassion* (of Jesus)', allowing themselves to be moved to a human and political acknowledgement – with important consequences – of those who can do nothing else but pray for the essentials that are their right.[15] This is a 'weak "authority"',[16] this kind that lies in the prayer of petition. It is precisely of this that God's weak authority consists, as it speaks decisively in the incarnate Word of God, Jesus Christ, the 'authority of the suppliant Christ' (Eberhard Jüngel).[17] It

---

14 JB METZ, *Memoria passionis*, 166.
15 Cf. *Ibidem.*, 170.
16 Cf. *Ibidem.*, 173.
17 Cf. E JÜNGEL, *Die Autorität des bittenden Christus. Eine These zur materialen Begründung der Eigenart des Wortes Gottes. Erwägungen zum Problem der Infallibilität in der Theologie*, in ID., *Unterwegs zur Sache. Theologische Bemerkungen*, Kaiser, Munich 1972, 179–188.

can not resist being rejected in the poor and excluded, like Jesus Christ himself. It is found at the same time precisely in this 'weak' authority of the Father, whose weakness brings his divine power to bear; Schelling, the great philosopher of German idealism, described it along the lines of 1 Cor 1:25 with the utmost theological sensitivity: 'The weakness of God ... can be seen especially in his weakness for man. But in this weakness he is stronger than man. His heart is big enough to be able to contain everything. If in creation, he especially demonstrates the power of his *Spirit*, then in salvation he demonstrates the greatness of his *heart*'.[18]

Speaking of God's greatness of heart for the weak and for people who become weak, that is, the compassion of his heart [*Barm-herzigkeit*], which is known as *misericordia* in Latin, brings us back to the central idea we find in Pope Francis' discourse about God. In no. 16 of *MeM*, he writes:

---

18 FWJ SCHELLING, *Philosophie der Offenbarung. Zweiter Band, Ausgewählte Werke*, Wissenschaftliche Buchgesellschaft, Darmstadt 1974, 26. Julia Knop's important reference to Seneca's *De clementia* makes Schelling's formulation even more important than it already is with its evocation of 1 Cor 1:25. Seneca contrasts mercy (*misericordia*) to the clemency (*clementia*) of a powerful ruler which he can exercise when he wants to. Compassion, however, is – or becomes – weak, insofar as it is affected and emotionally moved by the misery of those he has compassion on (Cf. *De clementia* II.6). It is precisely this being moved which is what Pope Francis is talking about in his language about mercy. For him, mercy is the antithesis to a culture of uninvolved indifference and hard-heartedness; cf. FRANCIS, *The Name of God is Mercy. A conversation with Andrea Tornielli*, Random House, New York 2016 (for this indication too I am grateful to J KNOP, *Gottes Erbarmen denken*, cit., 401).

> Mercy renews and redeems because it is the meeting of two hearts: the heart of God who comes to meet the human heart. The latter is warmed and healed by the former. Our hearts of stone become hearts of flesh (cf. Ezek 36:26) capable of love despite our sinfulness. I come to realize that I am truly a "new creation" (Gal 6:15): I am loved, therefore I exist; I am forgiven, therefore I am reborn; I have been shown mercy, therefore I have become a vessel of mercy.

The Apostolic Letter with which he concludes the Extraordinary Jubilee Year of Mercy has mercy toward sinners as its special theme. The reference to Ezek 36:26, nevertheless, broadens this perspective, such that attention is given to the discouraged, the exiled and excluded to whom this prophetic text is addressed in the first place: those deported to Babylon, and along with them all the marginalized and discouraged people of our own time for whom God has a 'large heart', and a 'weakness', and that he wants to bring to the attention of those who, so often, and with grave consequences, have pretended not to see them and hear them. God's *mercy* wants to be shared; it is shown to human beings – including and especially the poor and the marginalized – but *not without human beings*.[19]

---

19 Augustine drew attention to this divine 'logic' of the *not without*; Thomas Aquinas quoted Augustine thus: 'He Who created thee without thee, will not justify thee without thee' (THOMAS AQUINAS, *Summa theologica* III, q. 84, a.5 *corpus*; AUGUSTINUS, *Sermo 169*, c-11, no.13). Perhaps today this sentence can be translated thus: He who created you without you, but has

This biblical belief in God remains weak and open to dispute, plagued by complaints and questions as to why God's weakness for man remains so 'weak' in the history of suffering and oppression; as to why it reaches so few people and redeems them out of generosity, out of a mercy rich in consequences for those who suffer, out of a *compassion* that wants to actively change their suffering. And believers remain under pressure from the question as to why God's creation is so overwhelmingly dominated the power of sin, such that *compassion* often seems powerless in touching the misery of all those who are humiliated by it or become its accomplices. It is the question of how redemption can be achieved for people, of how God's weakness for human beings can so powerfully change people's lives in this world, so that those who are abandoned to the power of sin can be saved through God's mercy. Our attention needs to be given to this question, but first we need to clarify why it is essential to speak of God's mercy, and how Pope Francis speaks of it with biblical precision.

you share in the process of your continual (re)-creation, will show mercy to you and all human beings but not without you.

CHAPTER 6
GOD'S MERCY IS THE SOUL OF JUSTICE[1]

In a central passage, *Misericordiae Vultus* (*MV*) quotes Psalm 136 (*MV*, no. 7), which praises the great deeds of YHWH in creation and salvation, confirming his steadfast fidelity. Each verse is followed by a refrain: 'For his mercy endures forever' – 'From generation to generation, it embraces all those who trust in him and it changes them, by bestowing a share in his very life' he says in *Misericordia et Misera* (*MeM*, no. 2), continuing the refrain of Psalm 136. The word 'mercy' no longer belongs to common speech. It translates the Hebrew word *ḥesed*. This Hebrew word associates generosity and the attention of the heart, which not only reciprocates a benefit received, but also seeks to say something 'that goes beyond the common notions of rights and obligations' and is determined by warmth: 'It is the unexpected, something one cannot really count on.'[2] But in

---

1 On the theme of justice and God's mercy cf. The overall synthesis prepared by D. Ansorge, *Gerechtigkeit und Barmherzigkeit. Die Dramatik von Vergebung und Versöhnung in bibeltheologischer, theologiegeschichtlicher und philosophiegeschichtlicher Perspektive*, Herder, Freiburg-Basel-Wien 2009.

2 HJ Stoebe, *ḥesed* = *bontà* in Italian, *kindness* in English in E. Jenni-C. Westermann (eds.), *Theologisches Handwörterbuch zum Alten Testament*, Gütersloher Verlagshaus, Gütersloh 1971, 761–768, here 762. Or in Italian the *Dizionario teologico dell'Antico Testamento*, Marietti, Turin, Vol 1, 525-532.

the case of YHWH it already happens from the beginning and is constantly renewed, so that one can say by way of praise that his ḥesed lasts forever.

There is one word that derives from nineteenth-century European usage, but which seems extraordinarily appropriate in today's theological context,[3] and can translate this idea: YHWH proves his 'solidarity' from the beginning and nothing can dissuade him from it. And yet 'solidarity' still says too little: with his heart, YHWH stands with and within what motivates his ḥesed, such that it wins out even when the people's exceeds all bounds. Even when Israel, for its part, renounces its solidarity with its God, ultimately YHWH is seen to be unable to let go and abandon it: 'My heart recoils within me, / my compassion grows warm and tender ... For I am God, and no mortal, / the Holy One in your midst / and I will not come in wrath' (Hos 11:8a,9b). YHWH's solidarity is fuelled by compassion which binds him deeply to people and keeps him steadfastly faithful to his solidarity. Compassion gains the upper hand over aversion, his 'wrath', because it results from a bond in which the 'I am there for you' (Ex 3:14) outweighs the sin the people have fallen into. God is not a mortal being who would be trapped in feelings of revenge. 'God's being God is revealed in his mercy. Mercy is the expression of his divine essence.'[4]

---

3 Pope Francis speaks of solidarity as 'this beautiful and sometimes uncomfortable word' Ted.Talk 25 April 2017: https://www.ted.com/talks/pope_francis_why_the_only_future_worth_building_includes_everyone

4 W KASPER, *The Essence of the Gospel and the Key to Christian Life*, cit., 82

This is where the second Hebrew word root comes in, expressing the biblical understanding of mercy (God's) in a significant way: *rḥm* (as in *raḥamim* for example). The word recalls the womb, referring to the "'private room' in the nature of the human being" (cf Gen 43:30).[5] The word occurs repeatedly in almost formulaic connection with *ḥesed*, in a certain sense as its specification. It then seems to be defined by contrast to God's wrath, as his turning to forgive once more. And it expresses the 'emotional' side of YHWH's attachment to the human being, which, as it were, prevents him from turning away from sinners. Of course, the praise of Psalm 103 shows not only the close interrelation of the two aspects of compassion for sinners and compassion toward the oppressed, but also the semantic proximity to YHWH's lawful, refreshing justice:

> Bless the Lord, O my soul,
>   and do not forget all his benefits—
> who forgives all your iniquity,
>   who heals all your diseases,
> who redeems your life from the Pit,
>   who crowns you with steadfast love and mercy ...
> The Lord works vindication
>   and justice for all who are oppressed (Ps 103:2-4, 6)

YHWH gives sinners time to repent: his 'patient' solidarity should re-awaken and strengthen their good

---

5 HJ Stoebe, *rḥm showing mercy*, rḥm *Sich erbarmen* in E Jenni-C Westermann (eds.), *Theologisches Handwörterbuch zum Alten Testament*, Gütersloher Verlagshaus, Gütersloh 1971, 761–768, here 762.

resolutions, bring them back into communion with YHWH, *convert them*.⁶ The oppressed should learn how he is committed to their salvation; they are to experience his 'closeness'. Thus, it is true for everyone: 'As a father has compassion for his children, so the Lord has compassion for those who fear him' (Ps 103:13), those who conform to his existence.

This comprehensive understanding of God's mercy lies behind Pope Francis' texts for the Year of Mercy 2015-16. As the motto for this Holy Year, in reference to Psalm 103, he proclaims: *Merciful like the Father.* The mercy of the divine Father may be sought again and again, called on in our 'weakness' to move us to 'accept his presence and closeness to us. Day after day, touched by his compassion, we also can become compassionate towards others' (*MV*, no. 14). God's mercy is focused on our involvement, which he wants to elicit from us so that we can return once again to that 'communion of wills' in which God touches the hearts of his people and they allow themselves to be touched by his mercy.

The strong emotional emphasis which the Old Testament places on the root *rḥm* and which is then brought very much to the fore by Pope Francis, is a surprise: God has a 'soft spot', a weakness for human beings. He is inwardly receptive, accessible to the poor and those who have strayed through sin. So he does not have to be moved to mercy or 'motivated'

---

6 For the word pair 'patient and merciful', cf. *MV*, no. 6. The idea is completed in no. 21 of the same document: 'Mercy is not opposed to justice but rather expresses God's way of reaching out to the sinner, offering him a new chance to look at himself, convert, and believe.'

by people. They are already welcomed by him; and he goes in search of their hospitality to bless and reconcile them. It is in this sense that Israel offered sacrifices: not to dissuade its God from thoughts of annihilation, but to beg him to enter with his blessing into the life it had received from him but which was threatened by misery and sin, and to accept him and open itself to his presence.[7]

The metaphor of *God's accessibility* may allow us to complete the biblical understanding of God's mercy to some extent. God opens up; he is the 'place' where sinners and the oppressed find 'refuge'. He blesses them with his closeness; he makes them – as in sacrifice, for example – 'God-capable' so that they can live from his blessing and become a blessing themselves (Gen 12:2). People can reach him; he does not shut himself off from them in inaccessible distance to which only priests have access through the prescribed sacrifices. God's mercy manifests itself as his closeness which is blessing, which, of course, can only happen if he is allowed in, if people let themselves be caught up in his closeness, and transformed: *or put the other way around*, so that God's good will can bear fruit among people and between them, and his mercy may *dwell* among them.

---

[7] For this understanding of Old Testament sacrifices, especially in the post-exile era, cf. contributions which represent current Old Testament exegesis, in: B JANOWSKI-M. WELKER (eds.), *Opfer. Theologische und kulturelle Kontexte*, Suhrkamp, Frankfurt a. M. 2000. It can not be denied, however, that the influence of the aspect of 'appeasing the wrath of God through sacrifices' in Israel's understanding, as far as it can be noted from the practice in the Temple in Jerusalem at the time, is still very much felt.

This dwelling of his is not bound to rules and rites that purify and carefully define the most suitable place for him. Rather does it consist in the fact that he dwells *among human beings* and makes them instruments of his mercy,[8] collaborators in his justice: that they may 'walk humbly with [their] God,'[9] without always dwelling on what they saw salvation being dependent on. Go humbly along with our God, pay attention to the ways in which he preceded his followers, in ways that are unfamiliar and lead to the outer limits, to the marginalized: the ways of of mercy, inclusion, and being included in God's presence which is blessing. Once again we have come to one of the key themes in Pope Francis' discourse about God and at the same time have translated into contemporary terms a biblical and prophetic challenge, without which talk of God's mercy would remain superficial.

This challenge can also be found in biblical discourse about God's saving *justice*, on condition that we do not classify it within the traditional concept of distributive justice (*iustitia distributiva*). God's justice does not end in punishment which excludes one from his saving presence,

---

8   A sacrificial practice that seeks to ensure God's saving closeness through sacrifice is opposed by the prophets: 'I desire mercy, not sacrifice', attributed to Mt 9:13, to the tradition; it is a more indirect reference to Hos 6:6 and Am 5:21. *MV*, no. 20 cites this verse to address the horizon of faith regarding a justice that does not exclude sinners, but calls on them to enter into God's mercy.

9   Impressively dramatized is the prophetic opposition in Mi 6:1-8, where YHWH objects to the people ready to make any kind of sacrifice: 'He has told you, O mortal, what is good; and what does the Lord require of you but to do justice, and to love kindness, and to walk humbly with your God?' (Mi 6:8).

but in the mercy that seeks to bring people into [*hereinholen*] it – including sinners. It is a justice shown to people – sinners, the poor and the wretched – when they are freed from the desire for exclusion, and from being excluded; when, as happens in their bond with God, social bonds which bring human beings together in the good life are renewed and healed. To put it in contemporary language imbued with the biblical spirit, it is based on the justice of participation and empowerment, not on the justice of formal equivalence according to which the rule is: 'to each his due'. In this sense we should arrive at a point where no one is prevented from the participation worthy of the human being and excluded from the network of creation which enables one to live as a human being. Whoever prevents others from such participation in life, because he or she 'takes too much' or wastes or spoils goods that can serve others for enjoying a good life, who makes others victims of his or her greed and unscrupulousness, must, of course be stopped from doing this by enforcing a 'coercive' law based on sanctions. Victims are to be protected from the fact that power prevails over justice, that those who are stronger take no account of the rights of the poor and the weak to share in this justice. YHWH defends the right of the poor. He does not accept that they are treated as a '*quantité négligeable*'. His compassion for victims is not addressed to those who make them victims.

Injustice takes place as exclusion, as the denial of a sharing in God's creation which is worthy of the human being. Thus, the implementation of justice involves the restoration of the meaning of creation, the experiencing of the mercy and 'tenderness' which the Creator shows human beings in creation.[10] The mercy that brings people in [*hereinholen*] and makes participants of them is the 'soul' of justice; it should come to life in and through it. It is about a *balance of life* in which some do not take up room at the expense of others in life and 'push them up against a wall,' but where everyone finds room to share in the beauty and goodness of creation and where people can enrich one another's lives. Distributive or equitable justice serves this balance of life where everyone should have what they deserve. If formal justice becomes an end in itself, it promotes the myth of 'reward and punishment' in which there is a balance between action and retribution, making God ultimately responsible.[11]

Even for sinners who disturb this balance of life in creation, because they do not want to subject themselves to it, justice should happen in such a way that they are once again brought into the network of creation and play their part in it correctly. God has 'patience' with them. He calls them to repentance, so that they may be seized again by his goodness – by the goodness of his ongoing creation (the *creatio continua*) – and by trusting in God's creative good

---

10   Cf. *Laudato Si'* (*LS*), no. 84: 'The entire material universe speaks of God's love, his boundless affection for us. Soil, water, mountains: everything is, as it were, a caress of God.'

11   Paul Ricoeur take up this myth of punishment (and reward) in a profound and sophisticated way in P. Ricœur, *Interpretation des Strafmythos*, in Id., *Hermeneutik und Psychoanalyse. Der Konflikt der Interpretationen II*, German edition, Kösel, München 1974, 239–265.

will, which is also very specifically applicable to them, they may rediscover their own creative power.[12] He shows them his mercy through women and men who are at the service of his mercy, who try to make conversion appealing to them, and give them the opportunity to experience God's grace for empowerment.

The soul of justice is God's mercy. The 'innermost' aspect of his mercy is that he can *be moved*, emotionally speaking: he sees and hears the misery of his people (cf. Ex 3:7). But he is also touched in the depths of his heart and affected by the fact that Israel refuses his choice. Israel was meant to be witness to his mercy and justice and yet did not live by it. The Lord is deeply touched in his divine being by how his love is accepted – or comes to nothing. He makes himself dependent on this; he makes himself dependent on human beings … That's why he has this soft spot or weak point: people touch him in the depths of his being. Without them he no longer wants to be God nor let his benevolent plans be fulfilled.

This is the flip side of the mystery of his mercy, of his accessibility, the mystery of his *love*: 'authentic love also needs to be able to receive the other' (*AL*, no. 157) and does not give up hoping in the other. Love hopes all

---

12 *MV* looks closely at the relationship between justice and mercy. Pope Francis expressly warns against a 'legalism' that wants to restrict itself to the principle 'that everyone must be given what they deserve.' He points out that 'To overcome this legalistic perspective, we need to recall that in Sacred Scripture, justice is conceived essentially as the faithful abandonment of oneself to God's will' (*MV*, no. 20).

things (*AL*, no. 116); fixes its heart on the other. True love 'invests' everything so the other may love with him (John Duns Scotus). Thus, God invests human beings with an incomparable dignity: he can and *must* depend on them; they are not passed over, but are completed by God. He depends on them beyond any human anticipation and God's mercy does not abandon them, even when they fail to appreciate or they misunderstand their dignity: that is the tremendous tension in this mystery that faith may perhaps grasp but never resolve. Whoever understands in faith may perhaps also gain some light on the dark question in theodicy; just some light, which is much less than a 'solution'. Thus believers are obliged for their part to be patient with God[13] and to open their questions about God to this astonishingly hopeful question: how can it be that God allows himself to depend on human beings so much that nothing dissuades him from conferring the dignity on them of being his collaborators, his co-lovers? From a Christian point of view, the plausibility of this intuition about God is shown in Jesus Christ, the self-communication of God.

---

13   Tomáš Halík has dealt impressively with this aspect; cf T HALÍK, *Geduld mit Gott. Die Geschichte von Zachäus heute*, Herder, Freiburg-Basel-Wien 2016.

Chapter 7
THE FACE OF GOD'S MERCY

'Jesus Christ is the face of the Father's mercy. These words might well sum up the mystery of the Christian faith.' These are the words with which the first paragraph of *Misericordiae Vultus* (*MV*) begins, announcing the Jubilee Year of Mercy 2015-16. Without any doubt, they are the central words in the gospel of God which Pope Francis wants to proclaim to the world and the Church at the beginning of the twenty-first century. With these words he wants to say from a theological point of view that 'the mercy of God ... is not an abstract idea, but a concrete reality' (*MV*, no. 6), a revelation of the justice of the divine Father's mercy which is revealed *as it happens*. The primacy and the added value of reality over ideas, which, as a good Ignatian, Pope Francis constantly repeats, comes to the fore in the christological expressions of the biblical traditions about God. The many testimonies of the Bible *according to which* God is merciful, from a Christian faith perspective point to the mission of the Son, in which we see *how* God is merciful in a tantalizing and faith-binding way. Jesus Christ lives out the mercy of God the Father in this world, because he turns to the needy, promising them the salvation of the eschatological kingdom of God (see the 'Beatitudes' according to Luke 6:20-22) by the signs he works, 'especially in favour of sinners, the poor, the marginalized, the sick, and the suffering' (*MV*, no. 8);

and by 'his passion and death, conscious of the great mystery of love that he would consummate on the Cross' (*MV*, no. 7).

It is because the face of God's mercy shines through *in the crucified Lord* that Christians from the very beginning have felt challenged and repeatedly produced new attempts at responses. One idea was developed in the tradition of Augustine and Anselm of Canterbury through metaphysical and legal categories, an idea the New Testament found by meditating on the Servant songs in the Book of Isaiah, and rites performed at the Temple in Jerusalem. These served as a way explaining the meaning of the cross. On the cross, God's mercy conquers justice, since according to justice, sinful humanity deserved eternal punishment. God has his Son bear the burden of this punishment and the Son accepts it fully so that humanity may be spared and forgiven and thus be able to enter God's eschatological kingdom. Thus God's mercy finds a way whereby justice is served but God's mercy nevertheless prevails.

For many people this theology of the cross has become foreign to them, or even offensive. Reflections on the understanding of mercy and justice, based on the texts by Pope Francis we have referred to and which are the result of biblical reflection, can also open up other ways of thinking and believing. Pope Francis has not offered these new ways, but I can offer them, taking on the theological responsibility for this, though without claiming that they are the only ones that are practicable today.

Already in the New Testament, the Crucified one is seen as the one who takes up and carries out the role that the servant of God in Isaiah has for all humankind: to bear and take away what threatens to oppress the people. But first and foremost it is God himself who bears and takes the burden away from his people – their misery and oppression in a foreign land, the misery of sin through which God has become foreign to them. Deutero-Isaiah has YHWH pronounce an oracle of promise:

> even to your old age I am he,
> even when you turn gray I will carry you.
> I have made, and I will bear;
> I will carry and will save. (Is 46:4).

The goat on which the lot fell for being sent to Azazel and which, according to the Day of Atonement rite, is to carry away all the people's iniquities (Lev 16), is taken by Deutero-Isaiah as an image of the action of the servant of God and YHWH himself, bearing and taking away humanity's sins. The content of the image intensifies the key point in Is 46:4: sin and misery are not carried away so that they no longer oppress the people, but it is the people of Israel itself which is carried by its God, saved by its God. God carries, puts up with his people, thus showing a solidarity – brother/sisterhood – of the most moving and salvific kind one could imagine: solidarity with the oppressed who have no hope, with those who have been lost along the way, imprisoned within themselves and with no way out of their misery. He carries them on his shoulders so that they can 'come home', come forever to a place which is good for them, a place of salvation.

In the New Testament, Jesus is recognized as Emmanuel, God-with-us, (Mt 1:23 in reference to 7:14-17), who leaves the flock to find a sheep lost in the wilderness and when he finds it, he brings it back to the flock full of joy (Mt 18:12-14) so that it will not be lost, to the joy of his Father in heaven. There are many artistic representations of this good shepherd as he carries the exhausted sheep on his shoulder. A small chapel in the church of Ste Marie-Madeleine in the Burgundian city of Vézelay shows the 'traitor' Judas, who has hanged himself on a tree, on one side, and on the opposite side, Jesus the Good Shepherd, carrying the body of Judas across his shoulders. Pope Francis himself has drawn attention to this depiction.[1] Mercy endures everything; it is born of the love that bears everything and endures all things (1 Cor 13:7). The word used here in the First Letter to the Corinthians (*hypomenein*) is actually associated with the idea of placing oneself under something (subjection, but also endurance) in order to carry the weight (cf. *Amoris Laetitia*, no. 118). Jesus calls out to those who are weary and carry heavy burdens along the way and proclaims the gospel of mercy to them: 'Come to me ... and I will give you rest' (Mt 11:28). He is the good shepherd. He is good because he does what is good for the flock, and carries it on his shoulders in the most literal sense of the word.[2] According

---

[1] In an interview with the German weekly *Die Zeit* no. 11, 9 March 2017, Dossier.

[2] We find a moving interpretation in sermons by Martin Luther which speak of the reign of the Son, realized in such a way that he does not oppress us as ruler, but 'carries us on his shoulders; it is he who carries us!' So Christ's kingdom is borne 'upon his

to the Gospel of John, he calls himself the gate for the sheep, through which the one who is the true good shepherd in the Old Testament comes to them: God the Father, who seeks to come to them again and again as the merciful one and shows that he is accessible (cf. Jn 10:1-18). His Christ is testimony to this and lives it; the sheep hear the voice that they know so well, so that they open themselves to him and let him enter[3] – in other words this is his good shepherding and his lordship: 'Listen! I am standing at the door, knocking; if you hear my voice and open the door, I will come in to you and eat with you, and you with me' (Rev 3:20).

Taking up the entire burden and being caught up in everything to the point of collapse is not the best recipe for daily life. What we have here, rather, is an image of the hope for redemption: mercy on which one can unload the burdens of an almost unbearable life; mercy which bears what we cannot bear, what is intolerable. It is the image of hope from a God whose mercy is realized in his Christ, taking the unbearable on himself. On the cross, Jesus himself depended on being carried. There, it was the Father who carried him; he carried what his Son was laden with. The unbearable was carried, he bore what had to be endured so there could

---

shoulders.' 'Christians are people who lie on his shoulders, who trust him firmly and let him carry them like the lost sheep. To put it briefly, no one is a Christian who does not lie on the shoulders of Christ' (Martin Luther, *Predigten über die Christusbotschaft* (Sermons on the Message of Christ), Calwer Luther-Ausgabe 6, Siebenstern, München - Hamburg 1966, 65ff.).

3   This would be another way to express the act of *believing*: 'Believing means receiving God' (G EBELING, *Vom Gebet. Predigten über das Unser-Vater*, Mohr, Tübingen 1963, 45).

be hope; he bore sin and misery, so closely connected with each other, so everything did not become hopeless. This is what God takes upon himself; he supports us in his Son, so that we are not lost to his kingdom. In his Son he goes out into the wilderness of human life to pick up and bring in [*hereinholen*] the lost. The good shepherd goes to the point of utter abandonment, betrayal, death of desperation, rejection of God, to continue to save and bring back in [*hereinholen*] even in this instance. The sculptor of Vézelay expresses all this in his touching image. This, according to the Christian faith, is the mission of Jesus, the Christ: to go out, so that no one should be lost, to carry those he finds and to bear what they can no longer put up with. This is the ultimate challenge of mercy, in which the Son of Man and Son of God lives God's mercy and endures to the last, so that nobody will be left without God and without hope. Thus, Jesus Christ is the face of God's mercy, a face 'covered in blood and wounds.'[4] The liturgy calls him *Agnus Dei*: The Lamb of God who carries, takes away (*tollit*) the sin of the world.

The sin of the world: this is the spell cast by sin, the domination of a wicked will that does not want what is good for people, but works to spread the poison of mistrust and the breakdown of coexistence in friendship; the seduction of 'collaboration' with what is anti-human, inhuman, and poses

---

4 Thus says the Passion hymn 'Head covered in blood and wounds' ('O Haupt voll Blut und Wunden') by Paul Gerhard, inspired by the hymn 'Salve caput cruentatum' by Arnolfo di Leida in the thirteenth century.

an obstacle to God's good creation. This is the seduction of sins in the plural, which threaten individual human lives in their goodness.[5] The 'Lamb of God' is the 'sacrifice' of God Himself to remove this spell cast by sin from creation. It is the self-sacrificing, risking and 'exposing' of God himself in the world in order to free people of this spell, to redeem them for a life that leads to the kingdom of God. Christ's mission is to bring people out of the realm of the power of sin, to make them receptive to the life of the Spirit that comes to perfection in the kingdom of God. This mission arrives at its goal, and beyond, on the cross: on the cross, God's good will springs forth anew, so that human beings will wish to fulfil it together. It is sin which is taken away on the cross: it loses its inevitability because in the cross of Jesus Christ, God takes it upon himself and unites himself in mercy and solidarity with those who on their own have so little with which to oppose the power of the enemy of God and humanity.

This image of redemption cannot show up all the theologically important aspects of Jesus Christ's work of salvation. Thus it should – and could – become even clearer that God's mercy also includes a real contradiction, *confrontation*: the sculptor of Vézelay represents, so to speak, God's mercy *after* the catastrophe. It applies here to the desperate and the vanquished. Judas is carried upon the shoulders even in his ruin. But mercy seeks to 'interpose'

---

5 On sin in the singular,, the 'sin of the world', cf. P SCHOONENBERG, *Der Mensch in der Sünde*, in J FEINER-M. LÖHRER (eds.), *Mysterium Salutis. Grundriss heilsgeschichtlicher Dogmatik, Vol. 2: Die Heilsgeschichte vor Christus*, Benziger, Einsiedeln-Zürich-Köln 1967, 845–941, 886–898.

itself beforehand, so that things do not come to disaster. Mercy and prophecy are the two sides of the same coin. Where malice and contempt for humanity spread, mercy confronts them and calls them to repentance. It becomes 'hard', downright unbending, resists these things, so that people can hold on to it (mercy): to the testimony that things can be different – and must continue on so that the lack of mercy does not dominate and destroy people. Those who do not heed the call to repent ignore the merciful testimony of this opposition – or answer in their own way. Crosses and bombs speak a clear, desperate kind of language.

Still further questions and topics would need to be addressed to implement this view. The point here was simply to explain an approach to the mystery of the cross of Jesus Christ which leads to perceiving God's mercy in it, shown in its ultimate consequences, without seeing that mercy reduced to a simple amnesty which removes from sinners the punishment they deserve.

Chapter 8
MERCY WHICH PROVES GOD'S OMNIPOTENCE

Can and should mercy be accorded this central importance in the Christian understanding of God?[1] Pope Francis disagrees with this emphasis, more in the anonymity of the internet than in serious theological debate. If one knew the tradition being referred to better, the contradiction would not turn out to be so self-confident.[2] Here, however, just one point, but a key one regarding the doctrine of God, will be taken into consideration.

1 According to Cardinal Kasper it lacks an appropriate dogmatic appreciation of the subject. After reviewing the relevant manuals, he calls the result 'disappointing ... indeed, catastrophic" (ID., *Barmherzigkeit*, 19, or in English translation, *Mercy, the Essence of the Gospel and the Key to Christian Life*). For the last third of the 20th century, this finding can also be explained by the fact that the main emphasis of the doctrine of God was on love as the 'essence' of God. It begs the question of the relationship, from this dogmatic point of view, between this definition of his nature and the essential attribute of *mercy*. This could possibly lead to a readjustment of the doctrine of the God's attributes and generally make the distinction between God's nature and his attributes problematic. And it would probably only work if one has the metaphorical 'background' or keeps in mind the background of the discourse regarding God's attributes – and not mercy alone. Cf. KLAUS VECHTEL, *Mehr als Metaphorik? Überlegungen zum theologischen Stellenwert der Barmherzigkeit*, in *Zeitschrift für katholische Theologie* 138 (2016), 421–434.

2 Kasper's book, *Mercy, the Essence of the Gospel and the Key to Christian Life*, recalls important aspects of this tradition.

The ancient metaphysical doctrine about God developed in Christian theology in the first centuries, and largely followed by medieval theology, focuses on God's omnipotence. Seen as a paradigm, it is posed as a doctrine of God's essential attributes, distinguishing him as the *most Perfect One*. Beneath the level of these attributes, which are the highest conceivable and even more so,[3] any rational discourse about God's superhuman perfection would not be possible; and it would lose any connection with the human experience of perfection. Medieval Scholasticism proceeds from the perfection of his being as cause.[4] From this perfection the 'outwardly addressed' attributes of divine activity arise – the perfections of divine knowledge (foreknowledge, wisdom) and will (freedom, holiness, goodness, justice, omnipotence, faithfulness) – as well as the perfections of God's being in himself (being-by-himself, independence, spiritual nature, eternity, infinity, simplicity, immutability, cause of all being, original truth, uniqueness, transcendence, personality).

Omnipotence is first of all a perfection of the perfect, sovereign 'outwardly addressed' divine action. Nothing can inhibit its performance. In a certain sense it also marks the self-fulfilment of the divine and supreme being: that

---

3 Based on Anselm of Canterbury's argument by degree, according to which any rational discourse about God must be understood as 'that than which no greater can be thought' (*Proslogion 2*), nevertheless there may be conceived to be something greater than can be conceived, because God is greater than that which can be conceived (*Proslogion 15*).

4 Cf. THOMAS AQUINAS, *Summa Theologiae* I, q. 1-3.

unrestrained self-power [*Selbst-Macht*] by which and in which God is already perfectly powerful [*mächtig*]. He does not have to become who he already is; he eternally realizes what is possible about being God. The omnipotent power of his being eternally realizes the perfection of divine being as cause, 'inwardly addressed' – God is unlimited self-cause – and 'outwardly addressed' insofar as God can accomplish everything he wants in creation and history in the context of the other perfections of his being. In this sense, Aquinas, in *Quaestio* 25 of the *Summa Theologiae*, assumes that, by virtue of his highest perfection of being, God has the highest capacity to be an active '*principium*' which is in no way passive (q. 25 a.1 *corpus*). The infinite increase of power when one thinks of omnipotence is thus accomplished by the opposition of *active and passive*: as an increase of an uninhibited ability, which is not in any way hindered in doing what it wants[5], or more precisely, what it can want, because it is in itself possible, and hence what God wants would not contradict his nature. A will contrary to his nature (his being) would not be an orderly, perfect willing and therefore would not be worthy of God.

This idea leads to a series of subsequent questions that make the concept of omnipotence appear to be full of tensions. When omnipotence is conceived of as the unlimited potential for what is possible, the question arises

---

5   Cf. For example JOHN DAMASCENE's profession of fatih, *De fide orthodoxa* I, 8: 'We believe in ... a power known by no measure, measurable only by His own will alone (for all things that He wills He can).' Behind this formulation lies Ps 135:6.

as to why the one who can do what he wants has not always realized what he wants. Does God – pure 'reality' pure action (*actus purus*) – not always have to realize everything he wants? For the perfect self-power of God *ad intra*, according to Thomas, God is always what he can and wants to be in his self-fulfilment. But this does not apply to God's action *ad extra*. Here, God's will and ability are effective as performative power (*potentia activa*), which gradually realizes God's will in time. God's omnipotence is originally and essentially self-empowerment [*selbstmachtigkeit*] and therefore identical with his freedom. His freedom would in a sense be meaningless or eternally past – incapable of wanting what is temporally finite – if it could not put into action through will and through its capacity what is not yet realized. But does this reasoning help with the troubling question of why God's omnipotence does not now bring healing to people in their suffering and ruin? It does help overcome the lamentation of theodicy: How much longer? Why not now?

The argument sketched out by Thomas Aquinas leads to a further question for theology: not only God's omnipotence and freedom must be thought of as being identical in God himself, but also all the attributes of perfection of the divine essence which are distinct in human thinking. But is the inner logic of an unlimited ability really the same as the logic of the other perfections of God? Thomas himself refers to the perfections of the divine will: love and justice as well as mercy (cf. *Quaestiones* 19 to 21). How can one reasonably understand their coincidence 'in substance' with the unlimited power of the highest degree of the Almighty?

These are questions that concern Thomas Aquinas, but one cannot say that they are central to his doctrine of God. As if in passing, he remarks with surprising concreteness that 'God's omnipotence is particularly shown in sparing, and showing mercy', because 'the participation of [human beings in] an infinite good' is exactly what, for God, constitutes 'the ultimate effect of the divine power' (q. 25 a. 3 ad 3). Thus, in harmony with the perfection of the divine being, a concretization 'resonates' of the content of that in which the omnipotence of God manifests itself to the highest degree, and which is not touched by the conceptual definition we have given earlier of the idea of omnipotence. Actually, the fact that omnipotence manifests itself to the highest degree through forgiving and showing mercy, does not fall immediately into the logic of an omnipotent power. In any case, it does not automatically follow from the concept of supreme, unlimited power that it find its fulfilment in forgiving and showing mercy to the highest degree.[6]

Thomas reaches the concept of omnipotence by coming from the infinite increase of self-power. The question of *what* this supreme will wants precisely because of its perfection, plays a subordinate role. Should not God's omnipotence, in view of what he always and decisively wants, relate to the context of the perfections of God's nature and be understood

---

6 Thomas' idea could be interpreted in the sense that God's supreme sovereignty consists in being able to make grace prevail over law. Nevertheless, Thomas here is not referring to the universal sovereign's *clemency* (cf. earlier page 66, footnote 18). He is more concerned with describing God's supreme power as ability to have people share in his goodness.

from the love that *is* God? But how 'can' and does a God want to be omnipotent, who is inwardly determined and moved by the love that constitutes his nature? Are not love and power ultimately mutually exclusive? 'A love that can do everything, dominate everything and, as it were, automatically impose itself on the beloved, is no longer love, but simply a demonstration of power,' says the Lutheran theologian Jan Bauke-Ruegg.[7] And how can one say in some way that a love which 'acts out' through supreme mercy is 'activity' and self-power, seeing that it finds its perfection in letting itself be *encountered*?

With Thomas' idea of omnipotence it becomes clear that discourse about God runs into tension if at the same time we want to take account of the tradition of the metaphysical doctrine regarding God, and the testimonies of the Bible and the Christian faith tradition. Thomas expressly quotes the prayer tradition of the Church in this connection between omnipotence and mercy.[8] In a text dating back to the 8th century, the Sacramentarium Gelasianum, which is still in use today in the liturgy as the prayer of the 26th Sunday of the year, it says: 'Father, you show your almighty power in mercy and forgiveness.' The tension, which now becomes evident with Pope Francis, can certainly be understood as a fortunate theological combination.

---

7 J Bauke-Ruegg, *Was heißt: „Ich glaube an den allmächtigen Gott"?*, in *Zeitschrift für Theologie und Kirche* 97 (2000), 46–79, 75.

8 Pope Francis refers several times and in key passages to this connection between omnipotence and mercy as found in Thomas Aquinas, as for example in *Misericordiae Vultus* no. 6.

The metaphysical doctrine of God suggested that God's perfection should be understood in the sense of self-sufficiency and unlimited sovereignty, that is, the power to dominate (*potestas dominandi*).[9] In this conceptual context, mercy could not be of central importance. It refers to a different conceptual horizon, that of availability for and the ability to create relationships. Perfect availability and the capacity to create relationships would include wanting and creating what is *other than oneself*, being able to let the other be and 'control' a relationship that still reaches out to the other in its uttermost loss [*Verlorenheit*] and reluctance to be in relationship, thus giving it the possibility of discovering its profound desire to relate and to live in freedom. The absolute availability for relationships and the unlimited capacity to create relationships means God is able to come close to human beings in their misery and sin whereby they remove themselves from the web of relationships in ongoing creation. God can enter into this intimacy with human beings, and by virtue of this intimacy they are able to create relationships from the isolation [*Absonderung*] they find themselves in such that they are once again freely brought into the network of relationships with God. God proves to be accessible to the human being: his closeness opens up the ability to participate in God's creative power of relationship, the empowerment of grace, by which all the creative possibilities of human beings are challenged achieve

9 Here the decisive influence of the metaphorical "substructure" of the theory of divine attributes shows up clearly.

to the greatest possible realization. God becomes intimate by freeing others from themselves and giving them power. He takes part in their lostness [*Verlorenheit*], to give them a share in his creative power, to evoke a life and a love that cannot be overwhelmed and taken away by any other power. Participation in this inexhaustible and invincible ability to create relationships: this is the power beyond which a greater one can not be imagined. *Participation* in the hardships that plague human beings in their world through fatal suffering and the sin they deceive themselves with: that is how God comes close to human beings, sharing their burdens in solidarity with them.[10] He proves himself to be merciful and accessible to them, so that they can get close to him and be called to conversion. Those who allow themselves to be touched by God's closeness in the Holy Spirit, who over God's closeness in Jesus Christ, find themselves in a force field made up of relationships in which their own life is once more disclosed to them, since they can live it by cooperating in creation and it becomes viable with God and by bringing them into God.

So that would be the tension into which Thomas Aquinas introduces his interpretation of omnipotence as an essential attribute of God: if it were considered as self-

10   This dimension of God's mercy is not found much in Thomas Aquinas. For God, mercy is not a *passio animi*, which, according to Thomas, would not be compatible with the Greek metaphysical doctrine on God; cf. D. ANSORGE, *Gerechtigkeit und Barmherzigkeit Gottes*, 318 with reference to the commentary on the Psalms by THOMAS AQUINAS,, *In Ps. 50*, where mercy is understood as the goodness of God in his power to ward off physical evil.

power and sovereignty of the highest degree, an omnipotent God would only be self-sufficient – self-sufficient and independent, not hindered in any way in whatever work he would freely decide to do. Insofar as he is absolute being, he would always be everything he can be. Mercy, however, is the opposite reality to self-sufficiency: the merciful God wants to be open to and encountered by those who are 'close to his heart'. He wants to be powerful in their regard, with them and for them in the sense that their lives and their living within creation is saved and can flourish. This creative power is no longer power in the traditional sense (*potestas dominandi*). He does not wish to impose his power in a sovereign way, as the power of a ruler, or control the will of those he dominates, but wants to reach them inwardly and thus call them into their highest potential for life.

But we can ask ourselves: could God still be *omnipotent* if his power was aimed at empowering people, so that as people called to be co-creators, they want what he wants for the good of creation, freeing it and making the work of creation fruitful? Does he not continually fail because of the refusal of people through sin? Should one not expect that he will finally fail in his will for creation and salvation, if he is so decisively dependent on the cooperation of human beings? It goes beyond all human imagination to hope that the power of divine mercy will open the door to a future for those who have been afflicted by suffering, death, and sin, and who are in fact 'imprisoned' in it – to a future in which everything that separates people from God and his love will have lost its power. It is only in the venture of faith that this hope opens up and that we can say what Paul confesses with the certainty of faith:

> In all these things we are more than conquerors through him who loved us. For I am convinced that neither death, nor life, nor angels, nor rulers, nor things present, nor things to come, nor powers, nor height, nor depth, nor anything else in all creation, will be able to separate us from the love of God in Christ Jesus our Lord (Rom 8:37-39)

The 'omnipotence of mercy' will not allow that, should not allow it. Only from a distance can people grasp how God's mercy brings 'victory', why it does not have to be defeated by the powers to which it seems scarcely equal in this world and beyond. The Judas chapel at Vézelay brings the unimaginable into the picture: where no power of this world can reach, and where, by any human criterion, God's omnipotence finds its limit, that is where God's mercy reaches. When there is nothing more that can be done, and it looks as if everything is at an end and destined for disaster, that is where a good future opens up and shows the merciful accessibility of God, who gives up on nobody. The omnipotence of mercy gives a future where everything would seem to be without a future. A greater power cannot be thought of. It is much greater than what, all too humanly, can be thought of as power.

It is precisely here that the tension lies – the saving tension which, together with the central significance of mercy for discourse about God, enters into traditional discourse on the absoluteness of God: in human terms – all too human – the greatest power it is possible to think of seems to consist in being alone – dependent on nothing – and able to carry out one's will without any limitation. But if God is essentially understood from the point of view of his mercy,[11] then God's accessibility, indeed his openness and the openness of the love that he is, comes into play.

So, of course, the theodicy question comes up again. Faith in the merciful God constantly comes up against the world's lack of mercy. From a human perspective, there is little to suggest that God's mercy prevails. It seems foolhardy to hope beyond the powerlessness of mercy in this world and to trust that God's mercy is infinitely more powerful than the lack of mercy shown by the powers of this world. Jesus Christ is the face of God's mercy. We can see in him what mercy can do. For Christians he is the sign – which is at the origin of every sacrament – that God's mercy wants to become a reality in the world and that in his believers the world begins to be transformed into God's kingdom. What shines out in him is how he leads them to it powerfully – through the power of love and mercy which disputes the dominion of the powers of this world. In this sense, faith

---

11 It is most remarkable that the central interpretation of mercy for understanding God, emphasised also in Islamic theology, is contested just the same. On this cf. the important work by M KHORCHIDE, *Islam ist Barmherzigkeit. Grundzüge einer modernen Religion*, Herder, Freiburg – Basel – Wien 2012 and the volume by W KASPER-M KHORCHIDE, *Gottes Erster Name. Ein islamisch – christliches Gespräch über Barmherzigkeit*, Patmos, Ostfildern 2017

should not forget 'God as all-powerful and Creator.' If it were to forget this:

> we end up worshipping earthly powers, or ourselves usurping the place of God, even to the point of claiming an unlimited right to trample his creation underfoot. The best way to restore men and women to their rightful place, putting an end to their claim to absolute dominion over the earth, is to speak once more of the figure of a Father who creates and who alone owns the world. Otherwise, human beings will always try to impose their own laws and interests on reality (*LS*, no. 75).

Chapter 9
THE MYSTERY OF GOD'S LOVE: THE TRINITY

God's power creates relationship; it becomes powerful in relationship since it communicates the power of living in relationship by the power of God.[1] In this sense, we are talking about a power that *unites us with God*, in the beginning and from the beginning: it is the power to connect irrevocably with the earth and humankind and – against the powers of isolation – to integrate them into the communion of his saving and perfecting dominion. *Laudato Si'* (*LS*) sees the theological guiding perspective traced here as being rooted and expressed in trinitarian faith. The chapter headed 'The Trinity and the relationship between creatures' says:

1   I take this idea from C HEYWARD, *Und sie rührte sein Kleid an. Eine feministische Theologie der Beziehung*, Kreuz, Stuttgart 1986. (Appears to be only in German. For the complete collection of Heyward's work cf. http://www.columbia.edu/cu/lweb/img/assets/6396/Heyward_CFA51305PDF2.pdf). This theological concept of relationship of Carter Heyward's, however, seems to me in some ways to be problematic, such as when she writes: "I believe that God is our power in our relationship with each other, with all humanity and creation itself" (49). How can one say in biblical and Christian terms that he is *our* power in relationship! Carter Heyward's book nevertheless offers many suggestions for considering and gratefully receiving God's power in our relationships.

> The Father is the ultimate source of everything, the loving and self-communicating foundation of all that exists. The Son, his reflection, through whom all things were created, united himself to this earth when he was formed in the womb of Mary. The Spirit, infinite bond of love, is intimately present at the very heart of the universe, inspiring and bringing new pathways (*LS*, no. 238).

In this passage, then it speaks of the Trinity in that it spells out the three ways in which God calls the world into existence, joins with it in redeeming and liberating, and in inspiring humankind to set out on paths that Jesus Christ has pioneered, toward life in abundance – toward the kingdom of God. The passage also speaks of the order of salvation (Greek: *oikonomia*), portraying God's love as leading human beings to the fullness of salvation. Each of these three dimensions of the 'economy of salvation' is understood as the specific 'work' of one of the three divine persons, working in concert with the other divine persons to bring creation to perfection and save human beings. In technical theological language one speaks of the economic *(salvific)Trinity*. The secret of the economy of salvation is love, which is God and in which, in very human terms, he communicates himself, transcends himself. The 'basic attitude' of love is this going out of oneself (cf. *LS*, no. 208). This going out of oneself makes one receptive and accessible; by going out to those we love, others become infinitely important for those they love. They do not want to be without them anymore.

Can one speak of God and his love? Can one speak of God's going out of himself, given that for metaphysical thinking about God, nothing can be 'outside' God? Or should one say it like this: 'The universe unfolds in God, who fills it completely' (*LS*, no. 233)? Human language and imagination reach a limit here which we can and must overcome: in *metaphors* that express in intriguing ways how conceptual language transcends itself. Greek metaphysics, which was taken up in Christian theology, knows only the inner aspect of the Absolute, in which it is perfect for and in itself. God cannot transcend himself because he is always everything in himself that he can be and is. For him, there is no 'more' of self-transcendence, no 'outside' into which he could transcend himself. Otherwise it would indicate a lack he would be forced to overcome by transcending himself.

The experience of love of neighbour though, objects that it is a serious lack if we are unable to transcend ourselves. It would prefer to speak of a God who transcends himself not out of something lacking in himself, but because of *the abundance of being* that he wants to share and by virtue of which he wants to go out of himself in order to win over other co-lovers.

God's going out of himself in the economy of salvation, however, does not alienate himself from himself; it happens in a *self*-communication with which he fills those he goes out to with himself, so they can be his co-lovers. Thus, in the economy of salvation, God proves to be the divine reality who *has people share* (in himself) and who *shares* in the life of those who he wants to fill with himself so they may find salvation and fullness. He has creatures share in himself; each creature, therefore, 'bears in itself a specifically trinitarian structure,'[2] which shows up in the fact that the creature attempts to create a network of relationships. This trinitarian structure finds its fulfilment in human beings, inasmuch as they can be part of and share in the gift in which God gives himself.

Trinitarian theology soon appealed to this way of speaking about the trinitarian God in terms of the economy of salvation, to protect and more clearly express biblical testimonies of God's self-communication. It is God himself who communicates himself and has others share in himself, in terms of the economy of salvation. Ultimately, however, creatures are not just figures of mediation due to creation. If this is all they were, God would not be able to communicate himself and live as God with human beings, let alone have them share in God. But if the Son and the Holy Spirit are to be called God without any reservation,[3] how can biblical monotheism then be maintained, given a tritheism which abandons the unity of God? Theologians in the early Church used all their speculative power to preserve biblical monotheism in their trinitarian discourse about God. One could sometimes gain the impression that in doing this they had some precise understanding of God's inner workings and were able, as it were, to exactly describe the *Trinity of the immanent God*.

---

2   *LS*, no 239 with reference to St Bonaventure.
3   As the Nicene Creed states.

Current theology is aware that all statements on God as Trinity are limited: formulations that have to be and are weighed up, so that we can continue to believe that God shares in the human life of his Son – who is his equal – and that he has him share responsibly in his divine love in the Holy Spirit – who is his equal – while protecting this from human (all too human) misunderstandings. In this sense, a formula by Karl Rahner has received widespread approval, in which he states: 'The "economic" Trinity is the "immanent" Trinity and vice versa.'[4] The doctrine of the immanent Trinity ensures, to some extent, that we speak about God's self-communication in the right way, in the history of salvation: God opens himself in an intimate relationship with human beings; and he shares himself so that he may be believed as the one who has opened himself and made himself accessible to human beings in creation and in the history of his mercy. God's 'innermost' being is his 'outermost' being, his weakness for humankind, in which he is so much more powerful than all the powers of this world. God's 'innermostness' enters into his self-communication; he 'transcends himself' by turning mercifully to human beings. In this way he liberates those who are prisoners of sin and misery, in order to bring them into communion of life with him.

---

4 K RAHNER, *Der dreifaltige Gott als transzendenter Urgrund der Heilsgeschichte*, in: J FEINER-M. LÖHRER (eds.), *Mysterium Salutis*, Bd. 2, 317–401, 328. This work can also be found in English translation: *The Trinity*. Translated by Joseph Donceel, 1970. New York: Herder and Herder.

How this inward movement of God can be understood in human terms has been given much thought in the history of the faith. Two models have emerged. The Augustinian tradition has a 'monologue' concept: God is absolute spirit. Spirit refers to itself in two ways however: by becoming aware of itself and by affirming itself. God is the absolute spirit-reality who – before he refers to human beings, to be recognized by them and to embrace them with his affirmation – is completely self-capable and infinitely self-affirmed. Eastern theology understands God more as the origin and goal of all communion in love. He is himself communion in a sense that can only be remotely similar to human communion, however much it may be an image of divine '*communio*'. The three divine 'persons'[5] are so intimate among themselves that not only can it be said of them that they are united, but that it must be said that they are one, one God. God is self-communication in himself: of the Father to the Son and through the Son to the Spirit, the Spirit and the Son to the Father. The three persons are open to each other, so that each one fully participates in the other and is the other. What happens in God eternally, happens 'outwardly' to humankind insofar as it can happen to them as finite beings: God gives himself to them as the absolute good that flows out of himself; he communicates with them perfectly in such an intimate way that they can share in the divine *communio*.

5   Here we speak of 'person' not in the common understanding of people today – that is, as the subject of an individuals spiritual self-realization – but as an 'intrinsic reality' (in Greek, *hypostasis*) which is in perfect relationship with the other divine hypostases.

In his references to the mystery of the divine Trinity, Pope Francis connects with this Eastern Church concept, which was then adopted in the West by Bonaventure and Richard of St Victor. He states, 'The triune God is a communion of love', '*Trinitarian communio*' (*Amoris Laetitia*, no. 11 and *LS*, no. 239). God is in himself a reality of an eternal-original relationship, who communicates himself to creatures already in creation and gives them their being-in-relationship. He offers relationship and the forgiveness of his Son in order to reach out to human beings who have fallen into sin and misery, to once again call them into the divine communion. Through the Holy Spirit, he communicates the energy of faith, hope and love, so they may discover the ways that lead to God's kingdom and pursue these ways more or less consistently.

To open oneself to God's offer of relationship and reconciliation is, according to Pope Francis, to accept being a witness to the fact that this will be true also for the excluded and for those who exclude themselves: these are the ones whom they should witness to in the first place – by the Word of proclamation and even more through active testimony that helps overcome such exclusion. The missionary commitment to bring the *joy of the gospel* to the peripheries is not just to win over members for the Church, but – in the spirit of the Apostle Paul (cf. 2 Cor 1:24) - to be at the service of the joy of the people so that they will experience the divine will for relationship in a vivid and liberating way. For Pope Francis, the doctrine of God is no theological end in itself, but an introduction to life with God; with the God who engages those who live with him, so that no one is lost through lack of relationship with God and human beings, and thus excluded from the web of relationships of life to the full.

God's reality discloses to human beings the reality of their own humanity – and challenges them to place themselves at the service of humanity so that it may find its fulfilment in a life filled with God. From an authentically Christian point of view, to speak of God means to articulate the reality of God in such a way that this challenge can be heard; that the gospel which proclaims the availability of God may be able to create relationships, and that the God and Father of Jesus Christ who through his Spirit encourages us to believe, wants to inspire us to hope, to be 'ablaze' with love. To believe as Christians, therefore, means to be able to insert oneself into life, starting from God the Creator, God the Son who has become our brother, and God the Spirit, in the *communio* of the Trinitarian God, and it is also to feel called to the duty of seeing that no one is excluded or given up for lost when it comes to *communio* among human beings.

www.ingramcontent.com/pod-product-compliance
Lightning Source LLC
Chambersburg PA
CBHW052027290426
44112CB00014B/2416